THE STUDENT LEADERSHIP CHALLENGE

Activities Book

James Kouzes and Barry Posner
with Beth High and Gary M. Morgan

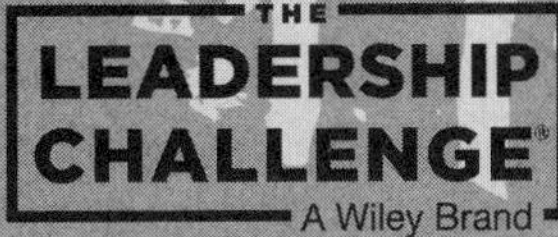

Cover design by: Adrian Morgan

Published by The Leadership Challenge®
A Wiley Brand
One Montgomery Street, Suite 1200, San Francisco, CA 94104-4594
www.leadershipchallenge.com
www.studentleadershipchallenge.com

For additional copies or bulk purchases of this book or to learn more about The Leadership Challenge®, please contact us toll free at 1-866-888-5159 or by email at leadership@wiley.com.

Wiley publishes in a variety of print and electronic formats and by print-on-demand. Some material included with standard print versions of this book may not be included in e-books or in print-on-demand. If this book refers to media such as a CD or DVD that is not included in the version you purchased, you may download this material at http://booksupport.wiley.com. For more information about Wiley products, visit www.wiley.com.

ISBN: 978-1-118-39010-8 (paper)
ISBN: 978-1-118-59972-3 (ebk.)
ISBN: 978-1-118-59965-5 (ebk.)

Printed in the United States of America
FIRST EDITION
PB Printing 10 9 8 7 6 5 4 3 2 1

CONTENTS

ALSO AVAILABLE

Books

The Student Leadership Challenge: Five Practices for Becoming an Exemplary Leader, Second Edition
The Student Leadership Challenge: Student Workbook and Personal Leadership Journal
The Student Leadership Challenge: Facilitation and Activity Guide
The Student Leadership Challenge: Activities Book

Assessments

The Student Leadership Practices Inventory® Self Online
The Student Leadership Practices Inventory® 360 Online
The Student Leadership Practices Inventory (LPI), Self Instrument, Second Edition
The Student Leadership Practices Inventory (LPI), Observer Instrument, Second Edition
Student Leadership Practices Inventory Scoring Software, Third Edition

Facilitation Materials

The Student Leadership Challenge Reminder Card
The Student Leadership Challenge: The Five Practices of Exemplary Leadership Poster
The Student Leadership Challenge: The Five Practices Individual Poster Set (One Poster for Each Practice)

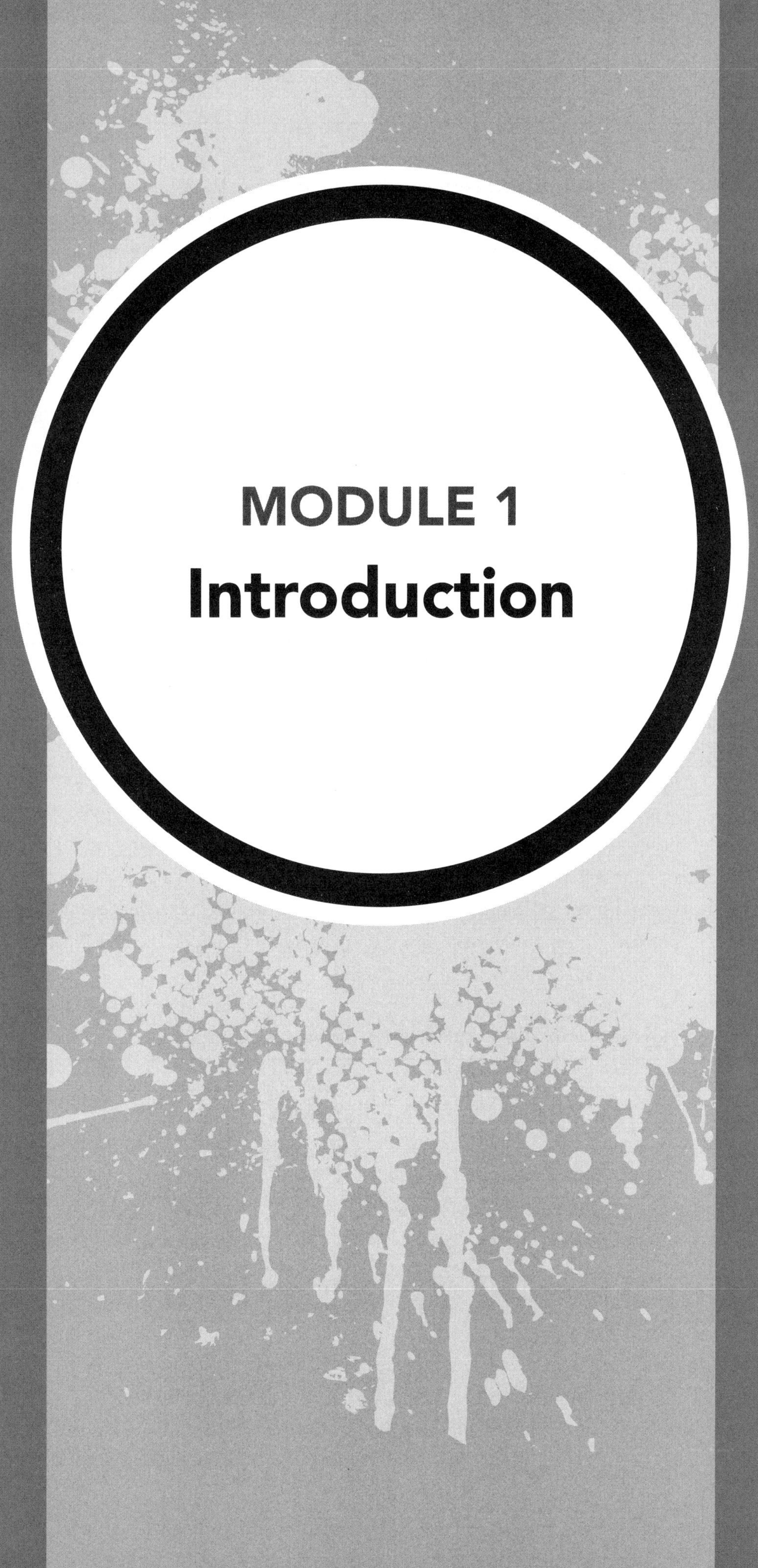

MODULE 1
Introduction

We know that practical experience is key to learning. There is no substitute for hands-on experience that enables students to deepen their understanding as they put the practices into action. *The Student Leadership Challenge: Activities Book* is designed to help you create those experiences for your students. Now in its second edition, this book builds on the research behind *The Leadership Challenge. The Student Leadership Challenge* is used by a growing number of educators and teachers who are committed to helping young people discover the leader within them.

Around the globe, we are finding educators like you who are helping their students tap into their leadership capacity, and this community of practitioners is growing. This book draws on the many wonderful ideas this community has produced and pulls them together as a handy, reliable reference for those who use *The Leadership Challenge* framework, research, and materials.

AN OVERVIEW OF THE FIVE PRACTICES OF EXEMPLARY LEADERSHIP®

The Student Leadership Challenge focuses on how student leaders get things done in organizations on their campuses and in their communities. The Five Practices of Exemplary Leadership model defines the behaviors that, when demonstrated with frequency, can bring about the best in themselves and those they aspire to lead (Figure 1.1).

The Five Practices of Exemplary Leadership are listed below along with The Ten Commitments of Leadership that correspond to the practices, two commitments for each practice. These commitments give a deeper understanding of The Five Practices and specify what leaders do to demonstrate them.

Figure 1.1 The Five Practices of Exemplary Leadership

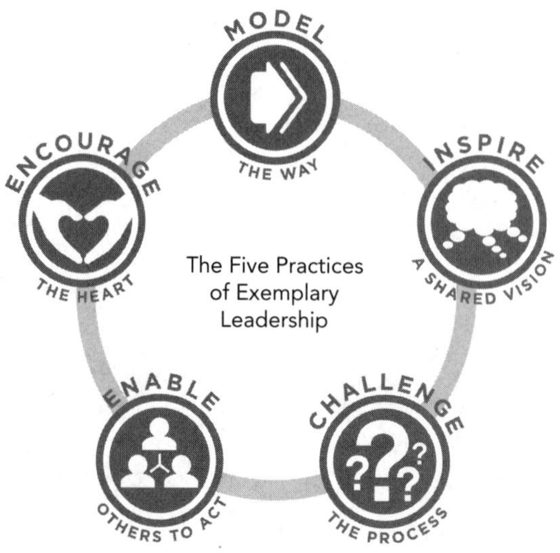

Model the Way

- Clarify values by finding your voice and affirming shared values.
- Set the example by aligning actions with shared values.

Inspire a Shared Vision

- Envision the future by imagining exciting and ennobling possibilities.
- Enlist others in a common vision by appealing to shared aspirations.

Challenge the Process

- Search for opportunities by seizing the initiative and looking outward for innovative ways to improve.
- Experiment and take risks by constantly generating small wins and learning from experience.

Enable Others to Act

- Foster collaboration by building trust and facilitating relationships.
- Strengthen others by increasing self-determination and developing competence.

Encourage the Heart

- Recognize contributions by showing appreciation for individual excellence.
- Celebrate the values and victories by creating a spirit of community.

Our research has identified thirty behaviors aligned with The Five Practices—six for each practice. When students demonstrate these behaviors with greater frequency, they become more effective as leaders. These behaviors are the core of *The Student Leadership Practices Inventory (Student LPI),* a comprehensive leadership development tool designed to help students measure their leadership behaviors and take action to improve their effectiveness as a leader. It is grounded in the same extensive research as the classic *Leadership Practices Inventory (LPI),* which is used in leadership training, executive development, and graduate–level programs around the world. The *Student LPI* is an invaluable tool for guiding personal leadership development based on an assessment of a student's current capacity to lead. In the listing of leadership behaviors that follows, the first iteration of the statement is the exact expression of the behavior in the *Student LPI.* The second iteration, in parentheses, is the way the behavior statement appears in the individual reports for the *Student LPI 360 Online* and the *Student LPI Self Online.*

Model the Way Behaviors

Statement #1: "I set a personal example of what I expect from other people." ("Sets personal example.")

Statement #6: "I spend time making sure that people behave consistently with the principles and standards we have agreed upon." ("Aligns others with principles and standards.")

Statement #11: "I follow through on the promises and commitments I make." ("Follows through on promises.")

Statement #16: "I seek to understand how my actions affect other people's performance." ("Seeks feedback about impact of actions.")

Statement #21: "I make sure that people support the values we have agreed upon." ("Makes sure people support common values.")

Statement #26: "I talk about my values and the principles that guide my actions." ("Talks about values and principles.")

Inspire a Shared Vision Behaviors

Statement #2: "I look ahead and communicate what I believe will affect us in the future." ("Looks ahead and communicates future.")

Statement #7: "I describe to others in our organization what we should be capable of accomplishing." ("Describes ideal capabilities.")

Statement #12: "I talk with others about a vision of how things could be even better in the future." ("Talks about how future could be better.")

Statement #17: "I talk with others about how their own interests can be met by working toward a common goal." ("Shows others how their interests can be realized.")

Statement #22: "I am upbeat and positive when talking about what we can accomplish." ("Is upbeat and positive.")

Statement #27: "I speak with passion about the higher purpose and meaning of what we are doing." ("Communicates purpose and meaning.")

Challenge the Process Behaviors

Statement #3: "I look for ways to develop and challenge my skills and abilities." ("Challenges skills and abilities.")

Statement #8: "I look for ways that others can try out new ideas and methods." ("Helps others try out new ideas.")

Statement #13: "I search for innovative ways to improve what we are doing." ("Searches for innovative ways to improve.")

Statement #18: "When things don't go as we expected, I ask, 'What can we learn from this experience?'" ("Asks, 'What can we learn?'")

Statement #23: "I make sure that big projects we undertake are broken down into smaller and doable portions." ("Breaks projects into smaller doable portions.")

Statement #28: "I take initiative in experimenting with the way things can be done." ("Takes initiative in experimenting.")

Enable Others to Act Behaviors

Statement #4: "I foster cooperative rather than competitive relationships among people I work with." ("Fosters cooperative relationships.")

Statement #9: "I actively listen to diverse points of view." ("Actively listens to diverse viewpoints.")

Statement #14: "I treat others with dignity and respect." ("Treats others with respect.")

Statement #19: "I support the decisions that other people make on their own." ("Supports decisions other people make.")

Statement #24: "I give others a great deal of freedom and choice in deciding how to do their work." ("Gives people choice about how to do their work.")

Statement #29: "I provide opportunities for others to take on leadership responsibilities." ("Provides leadership opportunities for others.")

Encourage the Heart Behaviors

Statement #5: "I praise people for a job well done." ("Praises people.")

Statement #10: "I encourage others as they work on activities and programs." ("Encourages others.")

Statement #15: "I express appreciation for the contributions people make." ("Expresses appreciation for people's contributions.")

Statement #20: "I make it a point to publicly recognize people who show commitment to shared values." ("Publicly recognizes alignment with values.")

Statement #25: "I find ways for us to celebrate accomplishments." ("Celebrates accomplishments.")

Statement #30: "I make sure that people are creatively recognized for their contributions." ("Creatively recognizes people's contributions.")

WHAT IS IN THIS BOOK

This book is full of activities, organized by leadership practice, to use with students of varying ages and in a variety of settings. These activities were gathered from many professionals who work with *The Leadership Challenge* and *The Student Leadership Challenge* around the world. (They are identified with short biographies in the "Authors and Contributors" section at the end of the book.) Our growing network of Certified Facilitators of *The Student Leadership Challenge* served as our main source. Although most are from the United States, our international partners are represented as well. As the use of these activities expands in new international settings, there will be lessons learned on how best to apply them in different cultures. We will include those stories on *The Student Leadership Challenge* website: http://www.studentleadershipchallenge.com.

Each activity describes the learning objectives, time required, materials needed, a recommended process, suggested questions for debriefing the activity and connecting it to The Five Practices of Exemplary Leadership model. We all know that debriefing and reflection are a crucial part of the process but also believe you will not feel limited by our suggestions. You know your students and are in the best position to identify the most beneficial opportunities for their learning. All activities include facilitator cues intended to address unique opportunities within the activity.

This introductory module also includes our perspective on why activities are so crucial to understanding *The Student Leadership Challenge.* We review The Five Practices of Exemplary Leadership model, outline what is covered in the book, and give you some pointers on how to use the content of this book to its best advantage. We also offer guidance on selecting and facilitating activities with students.

Module 2 covers orienteering, and modules 3 through 7 address each of The Five Practices. Each practice module contains an overview of the practice, our thoughts on its value for students, and experiential activities for developing the relevant knowledge and skill. Module 8 contains suggested movie activities. We believe that movies can be a highly effective way to help students translate behaviors they see on the screen into demonstrations of effective leadership, thereby deepening their understanding of the leadership practice in action. The movies we have included are by no means an exhaustive list, and we recognize that the list will grow over time as more great films are produced; the ones in module 8 are all tested and true depictions of The Five Practices.

Module 9 addresses the concept of commitment. Committing to ongoing deliberate practice is at the very core of *The Student Leadership Challenge* and requires specific attention. We offer suggestions and resources to help your students make the commitment to build self-awareness and deliberate practice into all aspects of their lives, for the rest of their lives.

The appendix gives a conceptual snapshot of the activities in a grid that shows them sorted by practice. Some of the activities can be used for multiple practices, and we have captured that information in this grid.

HOW TO USE THIS BOOK

Use this book to supplement and enrich the design of your class or program on leadership development. As you focus on each of The Five Practices, determine whether you have an opportunity and capacity to explore the practice more deeply by using an activity. If so, go to the relevant module and identify activities that address the learning objectives you have in mind. You can then choose the activity that makes the most sense for the time you have, the space available, and so forth. You can use the appendix to quickly cross-reference the activities and find the right one for your program or class. Be sure to review the facilitator cues included with activities for suggestions on how to customize the activity to make it most appropriate and effective for your students. Some modules offer suggestions on how to adapt an activity for practices other than the one for which the activity was originally designed.

GUIDANCE ON SELECTING AND FACILITATING ACTIVITIES WITH STUDENTS

Selecting Activities

Finding the right activity for your students starts with being clear on the learning objectives, that is, what you hope the student will gain from the experience. With those clearly identified, turn to the module for the practice you are targeting and review the activities. Consult the grid in the appendix as a quick reference for which activities are associated with which leadership practices. This may help narrow the field.

There should be enough information at the beginning of every activity to help you determine whether it will work for your situation. For each activity, we give its title, the learning objectives, number of participants, the amount of time required, materials and equipment needed, and room setup considerations. If all of these meet your criteria, review the step-by-step process. We have tried to keep the process section concise while still indicating the flexibility you have to adjust it to meet the needs of your students. We have also included facilitator cues throughout to present you with options and insights.

Facilitating Activities

Best practices are something that all facilitators identify for themselves over time. This book is not intended to be a facilitation guidebook. We wrote *The Student Leadership Challenge Facilitation and Activity Guide* to help you facilitate The Five Practices of Exemplary Leadership model effectively. As a supplement to that instructional guide, this *Activities Book* makes the assumption that you are a practiced facilitator with your own unique style. That said, we believe a few tips might be helpful as you explore the activities in this book. These tips are intended to serve as a refresher for some "golden rules" we trust will serve you well. They are listed below as do's and don'ts.

Do

- Practice the activities first. The directions and times are guidelines and may vary depending on your audience, situation, and facilitation style.

- Have your supplies organized and ready. A prepared start to any activity is always the way to go.
- Be clear on your directions (see the first point above). Someone who is dealing with a student population quite different from yours may have contributed the activity. Your directions need to make sense to your students.
- Create a supportive learning environment for your debriefing time. Students who feel confident to express what they learned from the experience will encourage others around them to do the same. Stay curious, and they will too.

Don't

- Underestimate time. This is a classic mistake that shortchanges the impact of these activities. If you take the time to practice them and manage your time well, you can avoid this pitfall.
- Overlook the opportunity to do these activities in places outside your normal teaching environment. Although most of the activities are described in that setting, they can be equally effective when applied in coaching sessions or as follow-up refresher activities. Use your imagination!
- Don't be limited by the words on the pages of this book. You know your student population better than anyone else, and we encourage you to put that knowledge to work to creatively get the most out of these activities.

The activities that follow will help you deepen your students' learning through experience. Adjust them as you see fit in a way that will support your students and their ongoing leadership journey.

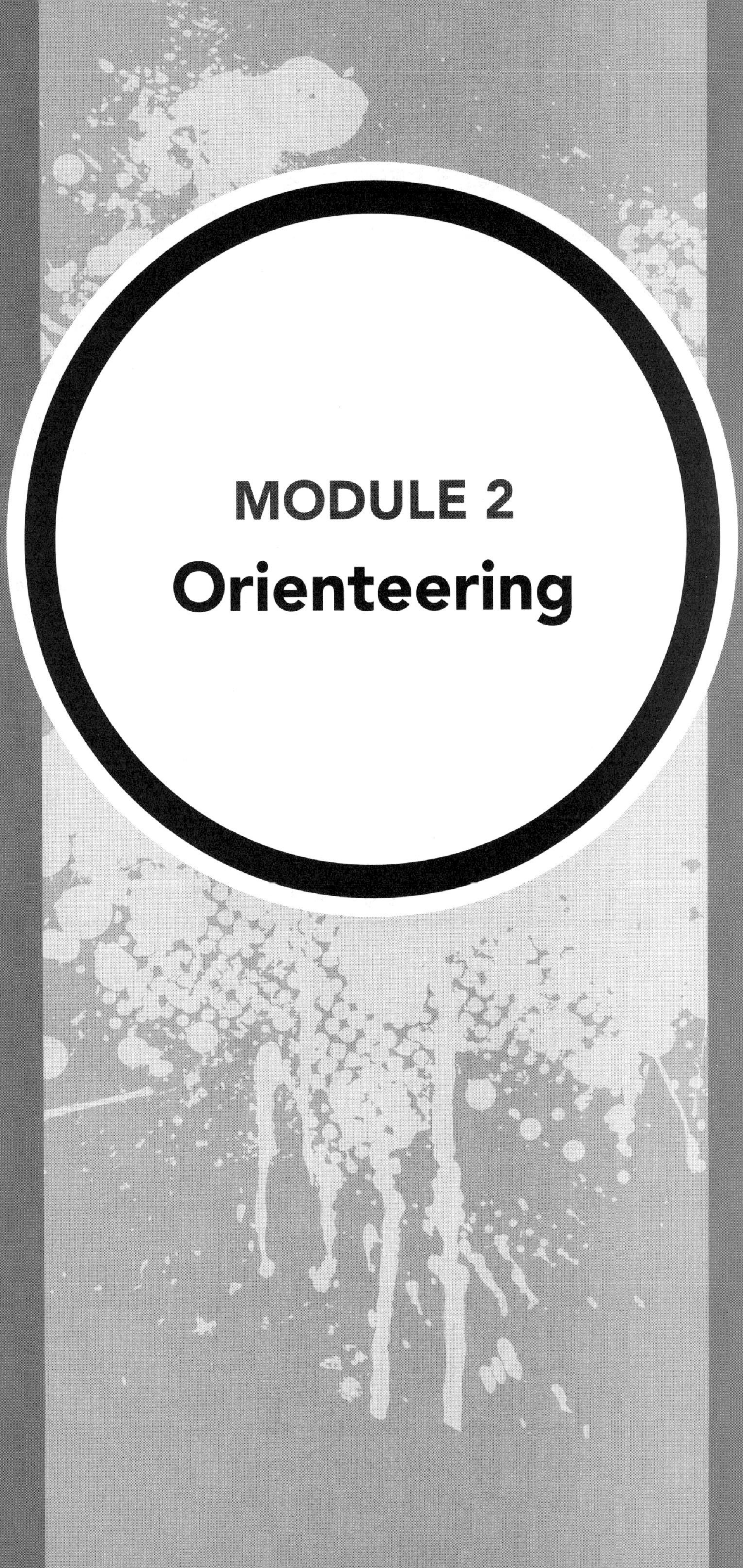

MODULE 2
Orienteering

A STUDENT'S PERSONAL JOURNEY TOWARD EXEMPLARY LEADERSHIP

Leadership is a journey, not a destination. And the conclusion of any successful endeavor is simply the beginning point for the next adventure. With each adventure, your students have the potential to grow personally, serve others, and have an impact on the world. It's a journey well worth supporting.

Meeting The Student Leadership Challenge is a personal—and a daily—challenge because in the final analysis, leadership development is self-development. We know that if your students have the will and the way to develop themselves as leaders, they can. You can help your students find the will, and exploring The Five Practices of Exemplary Leadership will provide the way.

The sport of orienteering is the metaphor we use to begin that process. Orienteering is a family of sports that requires navigational skills using a map and a compass to find the way from point to point in diverse and usually unfamiliar terrain. Each activity in this book can serve as a milestone on your students' leadership journey, a marker where deeper understanding of their capacity to lead occurred. Leadership is an ongoing process ordinary people use when they are bringing forth the best from themselves and others. When the leader in everyone is liberated, extraordinary things happen.

THE IMPORTANCE OF ORIENTEERING FOR STUDENTS

When students realize that they are on a journey that will unfold over time, their true learning begins. Accepting that they must continually call on the best of themselves and others is key. Holding a leadership position, such as team captain or student body president, is a wonderful experience, but it is short-lived. Once students recognize that each position is not an end in itself but an opportunity to proceed on their personal journey, they will begin to see the value in each experience in a new way.

All of this learning begins with recognizing their innate potential within to lead. The Personal-Best Leadership Experience activity that follows in this module is the cornerstone for this learning and for The Student Leadership Challenge. Before you begin to explore each of The Five Practices in this book, we strongly encourage you to begin with this activity. After that, we recommend that you explore The Five Practices in order. They are strongly connected, and although your students will be demonstrating the practices in their lives in no special order, their understanding of the logic behind the model is paramount. We highly recommend you have your students read *The Student Leadership Challenge* to deepen their understanding of The Five Practices by learning about other students who demonstrate the leadership behaviors embedded in the model. The book offers evidence from our research and that of others to support the concept that leadership is everyone's business. *The Student Leadership Challenge* provides real-life case examples of young people who demonstrate each practice and prescribes specific recommendations on what students can do to make each practice their own and to continue their development as a leader.

• • •

ACTIVITY: PERSONAL-BEST LEADERSHIP EXPERIENCE

The primary basis for understanding where The Five Practices of Exemplary Leadership come from is the Personal-Best Leadership Experience narrative. Completing the version of the original Personal-Best Leadership Experience Questionnaire that we present here allows students to find a standard of excellence from their experiences. In this module, as in the others, any required worksheets and handouts are included at the end of the activity.

This activity parallels the original research underpinning *The Student Leadership Challenge* and in that way helps validate the model for students. It is designed to help students define their personal-best performance or behavior as a leader. Once they know and understand what they do when they're at their very best, they can then know what it takes to act that way in all that they do.

Objectives

- To understand that leadership is within the capacity and experience of everyone.
- To understand what leadership looks like in action.
- To appreciate the similarities of leadership across varying contexts and circumstances.

Number of Participants

- Any size group

Time

- 60 minutes

Materials and Equipment

- Personal-Best Leadership Experience worksheet
- Writing tool

Area Setup

- It is important for students to have the time and space to reflect and capture their story. The room should be arranged to accommodate that kind of activity.

Facilitator Cue: Ask students to use the instructions and questions on the Personal-Best Leadership Experience worksheet to guide their thinking. Encourage them to be open and honest. Greater self-awareness will help them grow as leaders. Let them know they will be sharing their story with peers.

They should begin by thinking about a time when they performed at their very best as a leader. A personal-best experience is an event or series of events that they believe to be their individual standard of excellence. It's a student's own record-setting performance—a time when he or she achieved significant success while working with others. It is something against which students can measure themselves to determine whether they are performing as a leader at levels they know they can reach. They are not limited to times they held a formal leadership position. Their personal-best experience in fact may have happened when they had no official authority but chose to play a leadership role within a group, organization, class project, or even family situation.

For this activity, ask them to focus their thinking only on experiences during which they led others toward an accomplishment of which they are very proud. We use the word *experience* to mean any kind of project or undertaking that had a definable beginning and end. It might have lasted a few weeks, a few months, or even a few years, but it was something that occurred within a specific period of time.

Here are some things to ask students to think about when they are selecting their personal best-leadership experience:

- It could have taken place recently or long ago. It is defined as a time when they felt they performed at their very best as a leader.
- They could have been the official leader, or they could have emerged as the informal leader of a group. They might have been a volunteer or even a member of a temporary group.
- The experience could have been when they were part of a community group, a club, a professional organization, a sports team, or at school. It could have taken place in a workplace or in a nonwork setting.

Process

1. Have students describe their personal-best leadership experience (focus on a single experience) and ask them to answer these questions:
   - When did it happen? How long did it last?
   - What was your role? Who else was involved?
   - What feelings did you have prior to and during the experience?
   - Did you initiate the experience, or did someone else? How did you emerge as the leader? What were the results of the experience?
2. Ask students to list actions they took as a leader that made a difference by answering the following questions:
   - What actions did you personally take from a leadership perspective?
   - How did you convince others to do things differently than they had been doing them?
   - What did you do to demonstrate your own commitment to the project or undertaking?
   - What did you do to make sure everyone understood the purpose or goal?
   - What did you or others do to overcome any major challenges or setbacks?
   - What did you do to engage others and get them to participate fully?
   - Based on what you did or said, what other extraordinary actions did your group members take?
   - How did you recognize progress and make sure people felt good about being part of this effort?
3. Summarize what you consider to be the five to seven most important actions you took as a leader.
4. Ask your students to share the context of their personal best experience with others in their group and the "content" of their key leadership actions (step 3). Are these lessons they might share as advice to others about becoming an exemplary leader?
5. Once they have completed writing their personal-best leadership experience, ask the students to share their experience, including key leadership actions and lessons learned, with other students. After everyone in the group has shared, the students should discuss what they heard about what leadership looks like in action (irrespective of context or personal characteristics). Have them reach some consensus about what actions are required to lead others to greatness.

Facilitator Cue: Encourage the students to listen to the others' stories and look for common qualities in them—for example, excellent communication, focus, doing more than what was expected, helping people feel part of the group.

Reflection and Connection to the Model

After students have shared their experiences and come up with a list of common themes, capture the results in some way so that you can go back to them. Later, after they have learned The Five Practices of Exemplary Leadership model, you can ask if there is anything from their stories that doesn't fit within that framework. Chances are there is not. This is a simple way to validate the model in their eyes and help students begin to explore leadership using The Five Practices as their compass.

This activity potentially ties into all of The Five Practices and all the Student Leadership Practices Inventory behaviors. As you explore each of The Five Practices with your students, ask them to reflect back on their personal-best leadership story. Chances are they will notice that they demonstrated some of these behaviors in their successful experience. For example, if you are exploring Enable Others to Act, you will discuss facilitating relationships. Ask them to think back to their personal-best leadership experience and see if this was part of what made them successful. Chances are good that it did. This is the best form of validation for young leaders.

STUDENT WORKSHEET: PERSONAL-BEST LEADERSHIP EXPERIENCE

The research to discover what exemplary leaders do when they are at their personal best began by collecting thousands of stories from ordinary people—from students to executives in all types of organizations around the globe—about the experiences they recalled when asked to think of a peak leadership experience, that is, what they did when they were at their personal best as a leader. That case-collection effort continues, and the stories offer compelling examples of what leaders do when making extraordinary things happen. As you begin to explore *The Student Leadership Challenge* and The Five Practices of Exemplary Leadership, we ask you to respond to some of the same questions asked of those who participated in the original research. It's called the *personal-best leadership experience,* and we believe it will provide you with an inspiring view of the leader within you.

Begin by thinking about a time when you performed at your very best as a leader. A personal-best experience is an event or a series of events that you believe to be your individual standard of excellence. It's your own record-setting performance—a time when you achieved significant success while working with others. It is something against which you can measure yourself to determine whether you are performing as a leader at levels you know to be possible.

Your personal-best experience may have happened when you had a formal leadership role, such as team captain or student body officer, or it may have happened when you had no official authority but chose to play a leadership role within a group, organization, class project, or even a family situation. Focus on one specific experience.

Step 1

On a separate sheet of paper, describe this leadership experience by answering the following questions:

- When did it happen? How long did it last?
- What was your role? Who else was involved?
- What feelings did you have prior to and during the experience?
- Did you initiate the experience? If someone else initiated it, how did you emerge as the leader?
- What were the results of the experience?

Step 2

On a separate sheet of paper, list the actions you took as a leader during this experience that made a difference, and answer the following questions:

- What actions did you personally take from a leadership perspective?
- How did you convince others to do things differently than they had been doing them?

- What did you do to demonstrate your own commitment to the project or undertaking?
- What did you do to make sure everyone understood the purpose or goal?
- What did you or others do to overcome any major challenges or setbacks?
- What did you do to engage others and get them to participate fully?
- Based on what you did or said, what other extraordinary actions did your team or group members take?
- How did you recognize progress and make sure people felt good about being part of this effort?

Step 3

Summarize what you consider to be the five to seven most important actions you took as a leader.

Step 4

Review the responses from the questions in steps 1, 2, and 3. What three to five major lessons did you learn about leadership from this experience? (These are lessons you might share as advice to others about them being or becoming a great leader.) Write them here:

Lesson 1:

Lesson 2:

Lesson 3:

Lesson 4:

Lesson 5:

Step 5

Follow your instructor's directions on how to share your experience, including key leadership actions and lessons learned, with other students using the notes you took here. Hearing other personal-best experiences will deepen your perspective on the limitless opportunities for demonstrating excellence in leadership. As you listen to others' stories, look for common qualities you see in the stories—for example, excellent communication, focus, doing more than what was expected, or helping people feel part of the group.

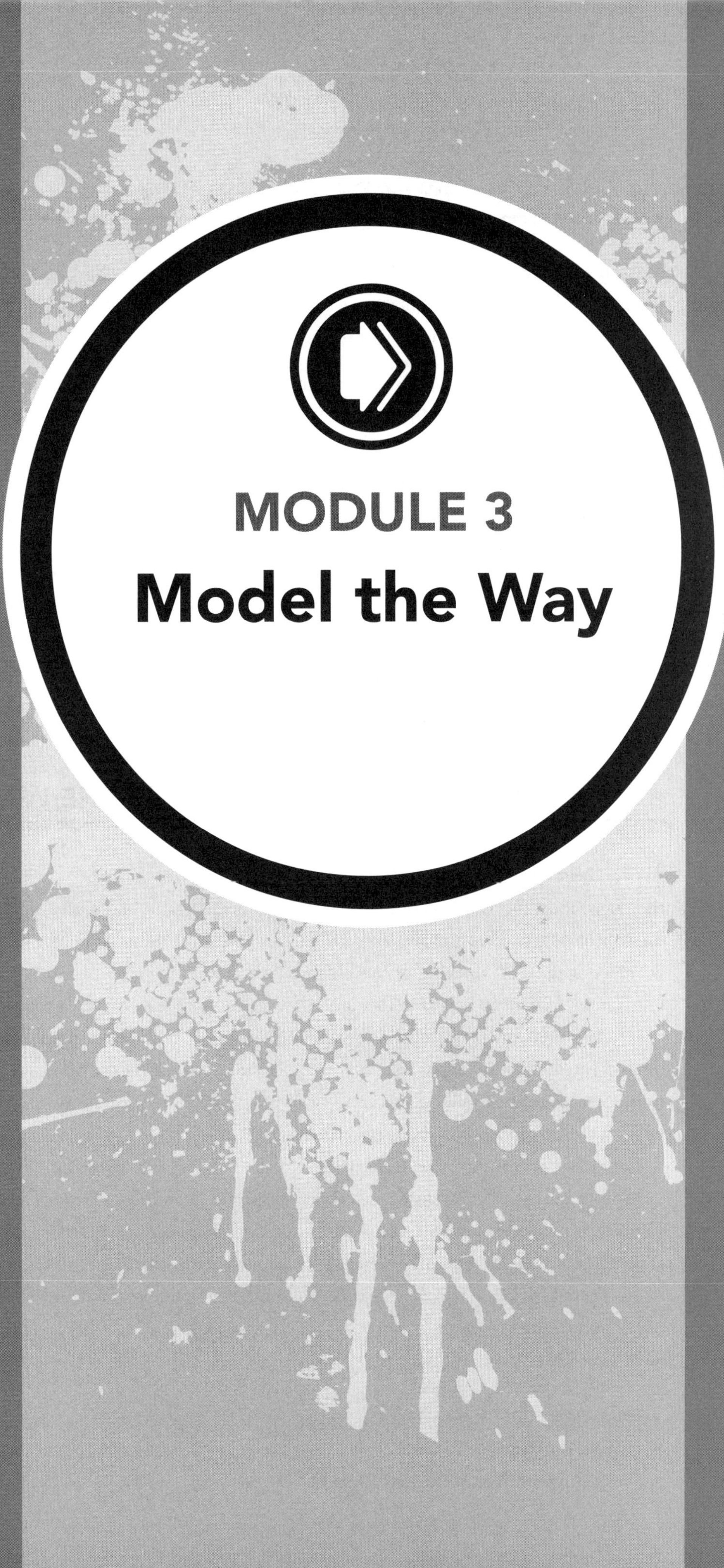

MODULE 3
Model the Way

PRACTICE OVERVIEW

Model the Way: Clarify Values and Set the Example
Leaders clarify values by finding their voice and affirming shared values, and they set the example by aligning actions with shared values.

The most important personal quality people look for and admire in a leader is personal credibility. Credibility is the foundation of leadership. If people don't believe in the messenger, they won't believe the message.

Leaders clarify values and establish guiding principles concerning the way fellow students, student groups, teachers, and advisors, among many others, should be treated and the way goals should be pursued. They create standards of excellence and then set an example for others to follow.

Titles may be granted, but leadership is earned. Leaders earn credibility by putting their values into action and living by the same standards and principles they expect of others. Leaders not only talk about the way things should be done, they show the way they should be done.

WHY STUDENTS SHOULD MODEL THE WAY

Above all else, people want to believe in their leaders and trust that they are who they say they are. Model the Way is about what it takes to be believable and authentic as a leader. These behaviors develop and sustain personal credibility, the foundation of leadership that we mentioned in the opening of this chapter. Just as building a house starts with a solid foundation, leadership begins in the same way. Students have to first lay a strong foundation before they can expect others to want to join them in building something extraordinary. The foundation is not the only consideration in building the house, of course: it must also have strong walls, a solid roof, well-placed windows, and doors for access. But without a solid foundation, the house won't stand.

Students who want to be leaders must make credibility a top priority. They must develop it and guard it carefully. Credibility begins with students being clear about the values they hold and ends with consistently aligning their actions with those values. Over time, this consistency helps others believe in them and trust that they will be true to their word. These activities will help students understand the value of Modeling the Way and offer opportunities to put it into action right now, regardless of whether or not they hold any leadership role or position.

Activities List

- Values on Display
- Modeling the Way in Current Events

- The Hefferlump
- You Want What?
- You Can Lead Anywhere
- This We Believe
- Legacy Day
- Vault of Values

• • •

ACTIVITY: VALUES ON DISPLAY

Submitted by Kimberly Hendricks La Grange

Objectives

Students will be able to:

- Identify their core values
- Reflect on how they are modeling their values as leaders

Number of Participants

- A group of 12 to 20 students is ideal, although the activity can be modified for smaller or larger groups

Time Required

- 45 minutes

Facilitator Cue: It is assumed that the participants do not know each other. A variation of the activity suitable for participants who do know each other is provided below.

Materials and Equipment

- Values on Display worksheet
- Pieces of card stock paper 8.5 × 11 inches—one for each student
- Watercolor markers (use those that won't stain fabric)
- Masking tape

Area Setup

- The area should be set up with tables and chairs, preferably in a U-configuration, plus an open area where participants can mill about.

Process

1. Each student receives a Values on Display worksheet, a piece of card stock, and access to markers and masking tape.
2. Ask students to circle the values on the Values on Display worksheet that are important to them. Following their initial review and identification of values, ask them to narrow the number of values to their top three core values.

Facilitator Cue: You may define *core* as "the values that help guide your decision making."

3. Have students select *one* of the three values they have identified, write it on the card stock, and tape the card on themselves or hold it in plain sight.
4. Ask students to move around the room and introduce themselves to three other students by sharing their names, their top value, and how they know this is a core value that drives their decision making.

Facilitator Cue: Give students three minutes for each introduction and help them manage their time. You might call out, "Switch," or have a signal such as a bell that keeps them moving.

5. Once they have completed their three introductions, have each student introduce one person they have met, sharing that person's name, chosen core value, and how he or she knows it's a core value.
6. You can use the following questions to debrief the exercise after the introductions:
   - How comfortable were you talking about your values with others? If you were somewhat uncomfortable talking about your values, why do you think you were? What makes it comfortable talking about core values?
   - In this activity, our values were certainly on display—literally! In your day-to-day life, what are the ways that you display your values through your behaviors? What would someone see if they witnessed you living your values?

Variation

If students in the group know each other:

1. Give each student the same materials.
2. Have them put the Values on Display worksheet out of sight after they have identified their top three values.
3. Each student tapes a piece of card stock to his or her back and is given a marker.
4. The students move around the room as described in step 4 of "Process," and for at least three other students, they write on that person's card the top value they believe that fellow student holds.
5. You may use the same debriefing questions as above. In addition have the students compare their Values on Display worksheet to the values they were assigned and ask:
   - Was there a good match?
   - Were they surprised by the values their fellow students associated with them?
   - If so, what behaviors might they be demonstrating that would lead someone to associate that value with them?

Reflection and Connection to the Model

People want to know who their leaders are: what they believe and what they stand for. The first step in becoming an effective leader is being clear on what values drive your choices and how you show yourself to others each day. Being clear is crucial for engaging others as a leader.

By living your values, you are Modeling the Way for others. As a leader, you are constantly being watched, whether you know it or not. Your behaviors influence others, often in ways that are not obvious. You must be clear on the values you hold in order to be able to consistently align them with the actions you take.

Student LPI Behaviors Associated with This Activity

1 "I set a personal example of what I expect from other people."

26 "I talk about my values and the principles that guide my actions."

STUDENT WORKSHEET: VALUES ON DISPLAY

Underline all of the values that are important to you. Then circle the three that are most important to you.

Achievement	Discipline	Independence	Responsibility
Autonomy	Diversity	Individualism	Risk taking
Beauty	Effectiveness	Innovation	Security
Caring	Empathy	Intelligence	Service
Caution	Equality	Involvement	Simplicity
Challenge	Fairness	Justice	Speed
Communication	Family	Learning	Spirituality/faith
Community	Flexibility	Love/affection	Strength
Competence	Freedom	Loyalty	Success
Competition	Friendship	Open-mindedness	Task focus
Cooperation	Fun	Organization	Teamwork
Courage	Growth	Patience	Trust
Creativity	Happiness	Power	Truth
Curiosity	Harmony	Productivity	Uniqueness
Customer Focus	Health	Quality	Variety
Decisiveness	Honesty/integrity	Recognition	Winning
Dependability	Hope	Relationships	Wisdom
Determination	Humor	Respect	Wealth

ACTIVITY: MODELING THE WAY IN CURRENT EVENTS

Submitted by Jerry Alva

Objectives

Students will be able to:

- Discuss real-world examples of Model the Way
- Recognize that leadership can be found in many places
- Gain experience working in small groups
- Keep up with current events

Number of Participants

- Ideal for groups of 20 to 25 but adaptable to almost any size

Time Required

- 60 minutes

Materials and Equipment

- News source
- Timing device

Facilitator Cue: There are many options for the news source, from local papers to global news outlets. Share your reasoning for the one you select. For example, if you select the campus paper, the exercise will then reflect examples of leadership on campus. If you select a global news source, the exercise will reflect leadership examples from around the world. If your students are on mobile devices, you can explore the variety of news sources they access and rely on.

Area Setup

- A space with options for working in groups, such as a room with small tables or enough space to move chairs around easily.
- If you are doing this activity online, you can establish virtual groups using social media.

Process

1. This activity is designed to occur after students have read the chapters on Model the Way in *The Student Leadership Challenge.*
2. Begin by reinforcing that examples of Modeling the Way can be seen everywhere: at school, at home, in their communities, throughout the world, and often in the most unexpected places. This will show students that all they need to do is look for examples.
3. Divide students into small groups; three to five each is good depending on the space in the room and the total number of students.
4. Tell students they have 15 minutes to find as many examples as they can of Model the Way in the media you've provided or their news source of choice that is accessible to all. The example can be an article, a quote, a photo, or even an advertisement.
5. Once the small groups find and agree on the best example, they will have 3 to 5 minutes to report to the whole group both a summary of the example and why they believe it is a good example of Model the Way.
6. Once all the presentations have been completed, reinforce that noticing the examples of Model the Way in current events is not just inspiring but helps to focus on the variety of leadership examples all around and therefore helps students to learn. Have students repeat this process for several sessions if possible.

Facilitator Cue: This can be a good online activity. Students can be assigned the task of finding examples and sharing on whatever community you establish.

Reflection and Connection to the Model

Model the Way is the foundation of The Five Practices model. It is important for students to connect the success, progress, and reward of being credible as a leader and being trusted to do what they say they will do. This activity allows students to see examples from many leaders in many different areas and reinforces how crucial Model the Way is in being effective as a leader.

Student LPI Behaviors Associated with This Activity

1 "I set a personal example of what I expect from other people."
6 "I spend time making sure that people behave consistently with the principles and standards we have agreed upon."
11 "I follow through on the promises and commitments I make."
16 "I seek to understand how my actions affect other people's performance."

21 "I make sure that people support the values we have agreed upon."
26 "I talk about my values and the principles that guide my actions."

Application to Other Practices

The activity of "Modeling the Way in Current Events" can be used for any of The Five Practices. When you help students identify current examples of Inspire a Shared Vision, Challenge the Process, Enable Others to Act, or Encourage the Heart, these practices become more real and more tangible to them. It also helps to reinforce that this is not just a model for leadership while a student but a framework that they can use throughout their lives, and circumstances.

• • •

ACTIVITY: THE HEFFERLUMP

Submitted by Rebecca Ford

Objectives

Students will be able to:

- Understand the importance of modeling the behavior they wish others to emulate

Number of Participants

- Any size group

Time Required

- 15 to 30 minutes

Materials and Equipment

- One flip chart and colored pens for the facilitator
- Colored pens or pencils and paper for the participants

Area Setup

- A classroom-style setup with the facilitator at the front of the room.
- Students will be drawing in this activity, so if they are not already at tables, they will need something to provide a drawing surface.

Process

1. Have the students seated facing the front of the room.
2. Stand at the front of the room and explain that on an expedition to the Amazon, you discovered a new species of animal, but you lost all but one of your drawings and photographs of this new animal. It is too small to share so you will be telling them what to draw by referring to your small drawing. Tell the participants that they have to do exactly what you say and draw exactly what you say to draw so they can then take the drawing of the new species and show it to the rest of the world.

Facilitator Cue: The object of this exercise is to have the students' drawings look nothing like the facilitator's small one, but rather be a mixture of the visual and the verbal instructions. The facilitator should have his or her own drawing facing away from the students so that it is hidden from their view.

3. Tell students that they cannot ask any questions during the drawing process, and reinforce that it is important that their drawing look exactly like yours and that it should be easy to do this because you'll be telling them all the same thing.
4. Start giving direction for drawing an animal that has the attributes of giraffe (see the facilitator instruction sheet, which has the picture on it), but give all the instructions as if you wished them to draw an animal more like an elephant.

Follow the cues in the facilitator instruction sheet, and be sure to say or do something vague or misleading in your verbal instruction to the students. The instruction sheet provides examples.

5. Go quickly, and if they start to ask questions, push them along saying something like, "I said no questions. Just listen and draw; everyone's hearing the same thing."
6. When you have completed the instructions, hold up your worksheet and have everyone hold up their drawings. The usual response is confusion or indignation. Respond in a way that gets students to articulate the problem and then reinforce the importance of being clear. Example:
   Students: You just said draw four legs! You didn't say draw four long skinny legs!
   Facilitator: Well, I held my fingers out and showed you. What's the problem?

Facilitator Cue: You are trying to demonstrate that as the leader of this exercise, you felt as though you were being perfectly clear; therefore, any misunderstanding is the students' problem because they didn't pay enough attention to their drawing.

7. Once students have focused on the idea that your messages were not clear, debrief with the following questions:
   - Why didn't your drawing look like mine?
   - Which meant more to you: my visual cues or my verbal cues?
   - What could I have done so that your drawings would look more like mine?
8. Reinforce that if people are going to follow leaders, those leaders need to be clear and consistent with their messages. Reinforce things they mentioned were confusing—for example:
   - It didn't help when I said, 'Draw a big head,' did it? More information such as, 'and round' or 'and pointy,' would have helped as you drew more. Right? We need to share important information that helps people understand context.
   - You said it would have been helpful to have either all verbal or all gestures, because mixing them up was confusing. As the leader of this exercise, it would have been more helpful if I had been consistent, right? That's what we want from leaders we are willing to follow.
9. Now ask them to think about themselves as leaders. Ask them to reflect on the following questions to explore the issue of credibility and consistency:
   - Can you think of an example of a time when your actions didn't reflect what you said you were going to do?
   - During that time, how effective were you in conveying what you wished people to do or the behavior you wished for them to exhibit?

Reflection and Connection to the Model

If you expect others to follow your example, your message has to be clear. In addition, your actions and behavior have to consistently reflect that message. It's part of the territory for a leader to tell people what to do, but when the leader's actions differ from his or her verbal instructions, people will get confused, and a lack of credibility and trust may occur. Remember that people have a choice in determining whom they are going to trust and whom they are willing to follow. A leader's consistency of word and deed is the surest path to gaining that trust.

Student LPI Behaviors Associated with This Activity

1 "I set a personal example of what I expect from other people."
6 "I spend time making sure that people behave consistently with the principles and standards we have agreed upon."
16 "I seek to understand how my actions affect other people's performance."
21 "I make sure that people support the values we have agreed upon."

Application to Other Practices

The "Hefferlump" activity can be easily applied to Inspire a Shared Vision. The disconnects between the leader and those who are receiving his or her message demonstrate how important the word *shared* is to the practice. If a leader delivers conflicting or unclear images, people are less likely to be able to engage with the vision in a way that is meaningful to them.

FACILITATOR INSTRUCTION SHEET: HEFFERLUMP ACTIVITY

Examples of misleading directions to give:

1. Say, "Draw a big body."
2. Say, "Now a round head."
3. Using your hand, dangle your four fingers downward and wiggle them. Say, "Draw four legs."
4. Pause for a while without saying anything, and then use your hands again, holding them up against the side of your head and waving your fingers, and say, "Draw big ears that stick out."
5. Say, "A long trunk comes from the head." (You mean a trunk-like neck, but don't say *neck*.)
6. Say, "Add horns."
7. Say, "Add stripes." (You mean spots, but that's a simple mistake, right?)
8. Say, "Add a tail." Use a big gesture and sweep your hand out from your back.

ACTIVITY: YOU WANT WHAT?

Submitted by Kurt Penner

Objectives

Students will be able to:

- Recognize their own values
- Recognize their expectations of coleaders and members
- Explore how they can more consistently act in alignment with their values

Number of Participants

- Any number of leaders and executives of student clubs, teams, and so on

Time Required

- 20 to 30 minutes

Materials and Equipment

- A large supply of medium-size sticky notes in two colors.
- Wall space to post the stickies; multiple flip chart easels can be used if wall space is limited.

Area Setup

- Movable chairs and tables if possible

Facilitator Cue: This activity works well as an illuminating exercise during the presentation of Model the Way. It helps student leaders realize there may be mismatches between what they are expecting others to do or commit to and how they are acting out their own commitments within the group they serve.

Process

1. Create groups of three or more, and space them along the wall or easels. Ideally mix up the groups so they contain leaders from different clubs or teams.

2. Ask the student leaders to briefly share their leadership context or role and clarify for them that this activity will be specific to that role.
3. Ask each group to use sticky notes to capture the behaviors or attitudes they are expecting or hoping for from their coleaders or team members. Offer suggestions—for example, the time commitments or response time they are expecting or how they hope to see respect, tolerance, or open-mindedness displayed. Each person in a group puts each behavior he or she identifies on its own sticky note and puts the stickies on display.
4. Have the groups take a few minutes to look at all of the posts the group members displayed and organize them because there may be lots of duplication.
5. Next ask each student to consider these questions: "Am I an excellent example within my own group of these things? Are there things I might be able to improve on or do more often?"
6. Using a different color sticky note, each student writes something concrete they personally could do to improve their own example-setting behavior and posts it next to the corresponding expectation.
7. In debriefing the activity, you can ask students if they identified something they felt they could commit to. Hearing these specific actions can be inspiring to others.

Reflection and Connection to the Model

Leadership begins with each person making a commitment to act in a way that aligns not only with his or her own values but with those of the organization he or she serves. Doing this is extremely difficult for those who are not clear on what those hopes and expectations are. Consider asking your students:

- How did you feel during the discussion about what you expect from other co-leaders? From members?
- What was it like to consider how your own example might be affecting the other leaders or members or how you might be in alignment (or not) with your own values and expectations?
- How doable are your action items: Overly optimistic? Challenging? Both?

Facilitator Cue: You can use this quote to encourage their commitment to action: "Setting the example is not the main means in influencing others; it is the only means."—Albert Einstein

Student LPI Behaviors Associated with This Activity

1 "I set a personal example of what I expect from other people."
6 "I spend time making sure that people behave consistently with the principles and standards we have agreed upon."
16 "I seek to understand how my actions affect other people's performance."
21 "I make sure that people support the values we have agreed upon."

• • •

ACTIVITY: YOU CAN LEAD ANYWHERE

Submitted by Lisa Williams

Objectives

Students will be able to:

- Clarify individual values
- Put values into action
- Identify actual situational opportunities to lead and specifically to Model the Way

Number of Participants

- Ideal for 10 students or more

Time Required

- 60 minutes

Materials and Equipment

- Notebook for note taking
- 3-by-5 index cards (5 per person)
- 3 bags (or baskets or buckets) labeled #1, #2, and #3.
- Whiteboard or flip chart and markers

Area Setup

- Have a table for the three bags at the front of the room that is easily accessible for all students and doesn't create a traffic jam when students come up to deposit their ideas.

If this is not possible, you may designate three students to collect the index cards and place them in the three bags, as well as distribute them for step 4.

- Students should be able to gather in groups of three to discuss the questions posed.

Process

Facilitator Cue: Students should have read the chapters on Model the Way in *The Student Leadership Challenge* prior to this activity. They should also have participated in a reflective values identification exercise.

1. Ask students to identify qualities that are important in a leader. Students may call out, raise hands, come to the board, or whatever else works in your instructional setting. Discuss with them how to clarify the list (e.g., there may be some redundancies.). Ask students to write one of these qualities on a 3-by-5 card and place the card in bag #1.
2. Review the six leadership behaviors for Model the Way and have each student write one of these behaviors on a 3-by-5 card and place in bag #2:
   - Sets personal example
   - Aligns others with principles and standards
   - Follows through on promises
   - Seeks feedback about impact of actions
   - Makes sure people support common values
   - Talks about values and principals
3. Ask students to identify different sectors in their school life—for example, classes, cafeteria, sports, arts, free time, commons, service. Ask them to write each on a card and put the cards in bag #3.
4. Working in small groups of two to three students, have each group pick one 3-by-5 card from each bag so they have a quality, a behavior, and a school sector identified. Have each group describe a leadership opportunity or challenge, or both, in that scenario. The situation may be real or hypothetical. Have each group report out how they will Model the Way in that scenario.

Variations

These variations are follow-up options for this activity:

- Create master lists of the qualities, behaviors, and sectors and post them side by side, allowing students to create a scenario that comes naturally to them. Ask them to commit to practicing it.

- From the same master list, have students identify a combination that does not come easily to them and try it.
- Reinforce over time how many occasions to Model the Way emerged when they didn't limit themselves to formal opportunities such as regularly scheduled meetings.

Reflection and Connection to the Model

Opportunities to lead occur all the time and all around us. The "You Can Lead Anywhere" activity helps students explore the opportunities in their current environment. To Model the Way, leaders must be able to align their actions with their values in all aspects of their lives, not just in their formal leadership positions. This activity helps students explore all sectors of their student life, enabling them to build in the deliberate practice that will help them become more effective leaders.

Student LPI Behaviors Associated with This Activity

1 "I set a personal example of what I expect from other people."
6 "I spend time making sure that people behave consistently with the principles and standards we have agreed upon."
11 "I follow through on the promises and commitments I make."
16 "I seek to understand how my actions affect other people's performance."
21 "I make sure that people support the values we have agreed upon."
26 "I talk about my values and the principles that guide my actions."

• • •

ACTIVITY: THIS WE BELIEVE

Submitted by Kurt Penner

Objectives

Students will be able to:

- Explore and clarify their own values and beliefs while listening and collaborating with another person or group
- Articulate their deeply held beliefs
- Speak on behalf of a group

Number of Participants

- Any number of participants

Time Required

- 10 to 30 minutes depending on the size of the group: the larger the group, the more time required

Materials and Equipment

- Flip chart paper
- Optional: Easels, which are useful if the group is large

Area Setup

- Movable chairs if possible to facilitate establishing groups

Facilitator Cue: This activity can be used to help students discuss topics of direct relevance to their group leadership (if appropriate); it can also be used with any other topic.

Process

1. Create pairs or groups of three, and have them spaced out in the room as far from each other as possible to minimize overhearing.
2. Give the students a general issue or topic such as "Violence in Sports" or possibly a more general topic, such as "Sports."
3. Ask each group to discuss the topic or issue and come up with a commonly held (and strongly held) belief or value related to the topic. If the topic is general enough, this should not take much effort. Of course, the larger the group is, the more challenging this could be.
4. Once the group has identified something (or more than one thing) they share in common as a deeply held belief, the object is for the each person to prepare a passionate declaration of this belief that can be shared with others in the full group/class. Have a trial run where each person declares the shared value in his or her own words, with passion, within the smaller group. Discuss the importance of passion with the whole group before moving to the last step.
5. Have someone from each group (or if time permits, each member) share the passionately articulated shared belief with the whole group.

Reflection and Connection to the Model

Leaders are passionate about their deeply held set of values. They realize that others are as well and that the only way to fully engage others is to understand and respect their values. Leaders listen carefully to the perspectives and ideas of others as a path to understanding their values. During those conversations, they do more than listen; they learn, allowing shared values and ideas to emerge.

Consider asking students the following questions:

- How did the process of sharing and listening go? How was discovering where you did [or did not] agree with others in your group?
- Were you surprised by anything you heard within your group?
- If you were the spokesperson, what was it like to speak for the group?
- How was this activity like [or not like] your actual leadership contexts?

Remind students that leaders need to reflect the values of the group, not just their own.

Student LPI Behaviors Associated with This Activity

6 "I spend time making sure that people behave consistently with the principles and standards we have agreed upon."
21 "I make sure that people support the values we have agreed upon."
26 "I talk about my values and the principles that guide my actions."

• • •

ACTIVITY: LEGACY DAY

Submitted by Andrea Junso

Objectives

Students will be able to:

- Align their identified values with everyday decisions

Number of Participants

- Any size group

Time Required

- 15 to 30 minutes

Materials and Equipment

- 2 to 3 sheets of paper and writing tool for each student

Area Setup

- Space that allows students to write and also to move to partner with another student

Process

1. Ask students to get a writing tool and paper ready.
2. Ask them to write a description (one or two handwritten pages) of a day in the future that they will remember forever. This will be their legacy day. They should answer the following questions in their description:
   - How did you spend your time?
   - With whom did you spend this time?
   - What was the most important thing you did that day?
   - What is the one thing that has to happen?
3. You should also indicate how long they have to prepare this description.

Facilitator Cue: You can have the students write as you pose the questions in step 2 or create a worksheet with the questions on it to guide them.

4. After each student has completed detailing his or her legacy day story, have them share it with a partner. After each partner has read the other's story and clarified any questions, ask them to write down, without talking, the top five values they believed were evident in their own legacy day.
5. Next, have students write down, again without talking, the top three values they heard in their partner's story.
6. Have one person share the three values they heard expressed in their partner's legacy day story. Determine how well they matched up with the values the other person meant to illustrate in his/her story. Reflect on the similarities and differences. Repeat the same process for the other partner.

Reflection and Connection to the Model

Leaders understand the importance of living their values. They make choices about how they spend their time based on their clear understanding of the values they hold and the values of the organizations they serve. They choose to spend their lives living their values, making choices each day that will help build their credibility with others. Consider asking your students the following questions:

- How did your legacy day compare to how you are spending your time currently?
- Are you spending time on what you value?
- Did your partner recognize your values from the legacy day you described? Would others recognize your values based on your day-to-day actions now?
- How did it feel to articulate your values to your partner?
- What opportunities can you take advantage of in your current role to align your actions and values?

Student LPI Behaviors Associated with This Activity

1 "I set a personal example of what I expect from other people."
11 "I follow through on the promises and commitments I make."
26 "I talk about my values and the principles that guide my actions."

• • •

ACTIVITY: VAULT OF VALUES

Submitted by Jean McClellan-Holt

Objectives

Students will be able to:

- Identify their organizational values
- Identify which of those values are most important to them
- Explore how those values affect their day-to-day activities
- Assess alignment of their values and the organization's values

Number of Participants

- Any number of participants; this activity is most effective for members of the same organization

Time Required

- 45 minutes

Materials and Equipment

- Vault of Values worksheet
- Writing tools for each person
- Flip chart paper
- Markers
- Sticky notes

Area Setup

- Chairs at tables are preferred; auditorium or conference-style seating is also acceptable

Facilitator Cue: This activity should be done after students have been through some type of values identification activity (e.g., the Values on Display activity in this module).

Process

1. Display the list of Sample Organizational Values and distribute the Vault of Values worksheet. Tell students to write on the top of the worksheet three personal values they have identified in an earlier activity (such as Values on Display in this module).
2. Instruct participants to reflect on the organization they are a part of (or select one organization in which they are a member if the group is not from one organization), and identify five values of that organization.
3. Have students work with a partner. Ask them to select one of the organizational values identified between the two of them and discuss by answering the following questions:
    - Why is this particular value important to the organization?
    - How does the organization exhibit this value in its actions?

Facilitator Cue: This can be done in small groups as well and repeated for all five values.

4. Distribute the Personal Reflection worksheet and tell students to answer the questions thinking about their personal values and the values of the organization.
   - Do the values of the organization align with my personal values?

Facilitator Cue: A common misunderstanding is that personal values need to be the same as the organizational values in order to be an effective member of the group. In your debriefing, this may surface. To help participants understand this relationship, say something such as: "Take a look at the list of organizational values. Some of these, such as Creativity and Quality may be a personal value, but others, such as Customer Service or Quick Response, are more clearly linked to the purpose an organization serves and the value they believe they bring to their members. It's important to reinforce that you want alignment of personal and organizational values, not a perfect match."

   - Can I accept the organization's values if they do not align with my values? If not, what are my options?

Facilitator Cue: You can have the students discuss this question with their partner, who might have suggestions for options. You can also do this as a large group debrief. Based on the discussion above regarding "alignment" versus "perfect match," you might ask for examples of an alignment that someone has identified. Can he or she give an example of a misalignment? It is important to review the variety of options available. Perhaps they can ask for assignments that are more closely aligned with their values, or they could introduce a value to the organization to see if is willing to embrace that value as a group. And they always have the option of leaving the organization in order to honor their personal values.

Reflection and Connection to the Model

Although the importance of organizational values—identifying them, sharing them, behaving as a team in a way that consistently aligns to them—is a driving force for Model the Way, for this exercise to be most effective, students should first be clear on their personal values. Model the Way begins with, "Clarify values by finding your voice and affirming shared values," which relates to understanding and articulating one's personal values. The Values on Display activity can be used in connection with this activity. Vault of Values is an organizational values activity to help participants gain a deeper understanding of the values held by an organization to which they belong and helps them explore the connection between individual values and group values. It also helps explore the challenges in consistently demonstrating the second commitment of Model the Way: set the example by aligning actions with shared values.

Student LPI Behaviors Associated with This Activity

1 "I set a personal example of what I expect from other people."

6 "I spend time making sure that people behave consistently with the principles and standards we have agreed upon."

21 "I make sure that people support the values we have agreed upon."

26 "I talk about my values and the principles that guide my actions."

STUDENT WORKSHEET: VAULT OF VALUES

Personal Values

Write three of your personal values below:

1.

2.

3.

My Organization's Top Values

Take a look at the Sample Organizational Values Table and select five that are more important in this organization. Write them below:

1.

2.

3.

4.

5.

Select one of the five values you identified, and answer the following questions with that specific value in mind:

a. Why is this value important to the organization?

b. How does the organization exhibit this value in its actions?

Sample Organizational Values

Diversity	Profitability	Duty	Creativity	Equality
Communication	Top Quality	Challenge	Quick Response	Efficiency
Achievement	Customer Service	Competition	Curiosity	Cooperation
Knowledge	Equality	Innovation	Prestige	Security
Effectiveness	Honesty/ Integrity	Visibility	Humor	Self-realization
Health	Cost Efficiency	Compassion	Mastery	Productivity
Helping Others	Education	Teamwork	Community Service	Wisdom
Quality	Trust	Exploration	Respect	Growth

STUDENT WORKSHEET: PERSONAL REFLECTION ON VALUES ALIGNMENT

1. Write below each of the organizational values you previously identified and indicate on a 1-5 scale (with "1" being not very well and "5" indicating very well) how well you feel that your personal values are in alignment with this organizational value.

   a.

   b.

   c.

2. Now that you have identified the degree of alignment between your personal values and those of your organization, write a sentence or two below as an explanation for the reason you gave the alignment score (1-5) you did. For example, there was a high degree of alignment (5) because I value taking responsibility, and the organizational value of "customer service" means that we stand strongly behind our products. Or, there was only moderate alignment because the organization says "innovation" is critical, but they are not always very understanding when experiments don't pan out as expected.

3. If you feel that there are areas where your personal values do not align very well with those of your organization, write down your options for dealing with this situation:

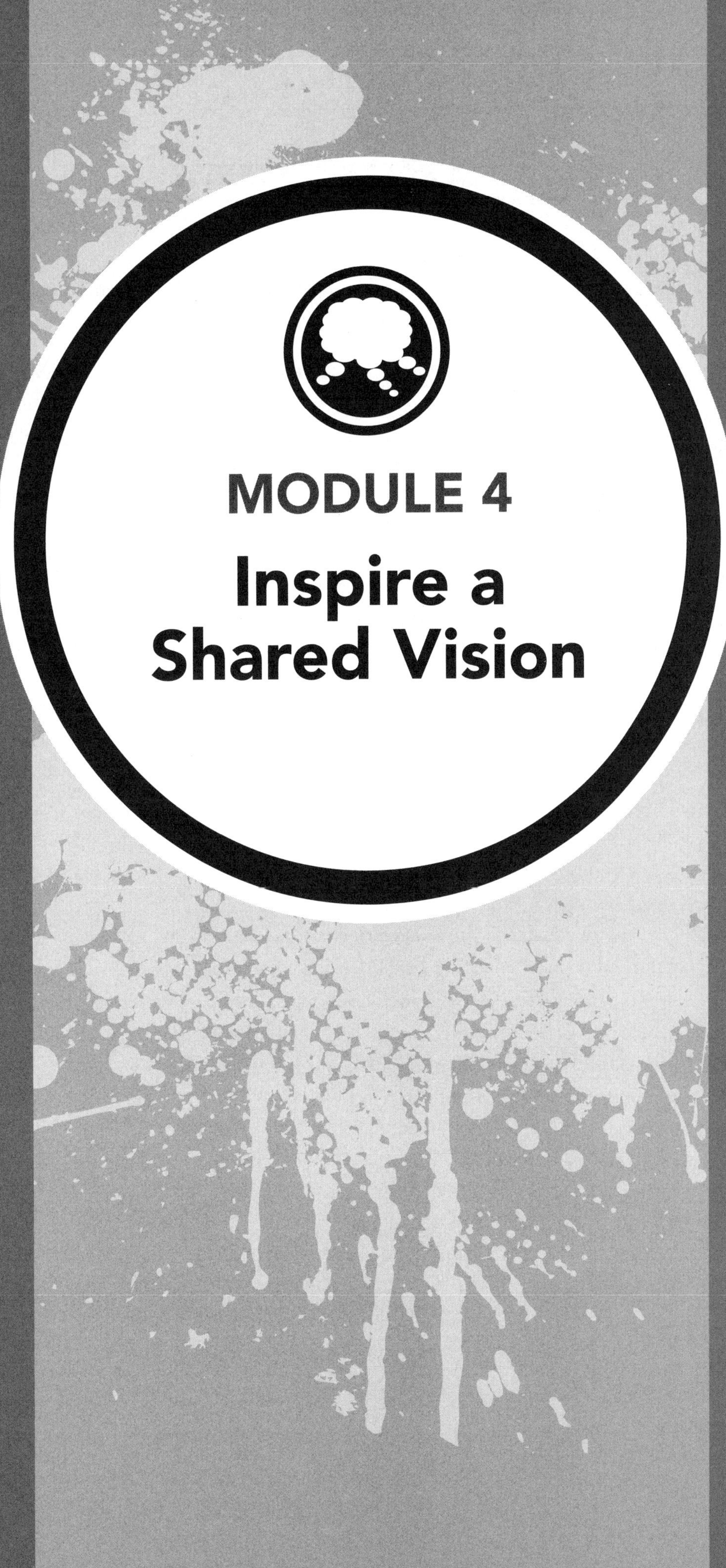

MODULE 4
Inspire a Shared Vision

PRACTICE OVERVIEW

Inspire a Shared Vision: Envision the Future and Enlist Others

Leaders envision the future by imagining exciting and ennobling possibilities, and they enlist others in a common vision by appealing to shared aspirations.

Leaders are driven by their desire to make a positive difference in the lives of others. They passionately believe that they can make a difference. They envision the future, creating an ideal and unique image of what the group or organization can be. Leaders enlist others in a common dream. They breathe life into their visions and get people to see exciting possibilities for the future.

WHY STUDENTS SHOULD INSPIRE A SHARED VISION

Exemplary leaders envision the future. They look ahead and imagine how they can change the ordinary into something extraordinary. Student leaders make sure that what they see is something that others can see as well. They understand that it's not just their own vision of the future that is important; it's the shared vision. When visions are shared, they attract more people, keep them motivated, and help them withstand challenges and setbacks. A clear, strong vision acts as a beacon of hope and inspiration for all, lighting the way to a better future.

Like anything else worth mastering, creating and sharing a compelling vision of the future takes practice, and it's a skill that sometimes students feel unequipped to develop, wishing to leave that part of leadership to others. But our research tells us something different: that leadership is everyone's business and that all students can and should develop the skills to share their visions of a better future. These activities will give students practice in creating images of what might be and engaging others in those dreams.

Activities List

- Going Up
- Word Pictures: Articulating Your Vision
- Giving Life to Your Vision by Reframing from What to Why
- Visualize Yourself
- Snapshots of Success
- Vision, Values, and Rock and Roll
- Sum It All Up
- Finish the Story

ACTIVITY: GOING UP

Submitted by Robert P. Carskadon

Objectives

Students will be able to:

- Practice sharing a vision
- Refine their vision to its essence

Number of Participants

- 10 to 20 students

Time Required

- 45 minutes

Materials and Equipment

- Masking tape

Area Setup

- A room large enough to mark off several small spaces approximately 6 feet square, the size of an elevator, on the floor with the masking tape.
- Create as many as possible in the space you have. The directions that follow are for a space that will allow only two or three "elevators." If you are able to provide enough elevator spaces to accommodate all the students, they can simply rotate partners after completing steps 2 to 6 the first time and then repeat steps 2 to 4 and 6 with new partners.

"Going Up" is adapted from "Inspire a Shared Vision Mingle" submitted by Darren Blonski for J. M. Kouzes, Barry Z. Posner, and E. Beich, *The Leadership Challenge Activities Book* (San Francisco: Jossey-Bass/Pfeiffer, 2010).

Facilitator Cue: This activity is intended to show how a well-prepared student can share his or her vision; it is not an activity to develop their skill in creating or communicating one. After talking about the importance of clarified values as a prerequisite in developing their personal vision, explain that leaders rarely have more than a short amount of time, approximately the length of an elevator ride, to initially inspire a shared vision (i.e., describe their vision clearly). In step 7, students begin to refine their visions for subsequent "elevator trips" (see the last question under Questions to Discuss with Those Who Shared Their Visions in Reflection and Connection to the Model).

Process

1. Have participants form pairs for each "elevator" space you have created.
2. Have one of the pairs move to one of the "elevator" spaces marked with the masking tape. Tell them that they will push the "button" to their floor and that one of the partners has only that time—45 seconds—to share his or her vision. Have the pairs decide which person will go first, and say, "Go."
3. At 45 seconds, say, "You have reached your floor." Have the students step off the elevator. The partner who listened has 30 seconds to provide feedback to his or her partner.
4. The pairs get back into their elevator to go to another "floor," and the other partner shares his or her vision for 45 seconds, the pair gets off the elevator, and the listening partner provides feedback on the vision for 30 seconds.
5. Pause the process and ask the students who were in the elevators (this may be some or all of the whole group depending on the space available) what feedback was helpful to hear. Collect a few responses so the whole group can hear. Next, ask them to think about what they would change about how they deliver their vision.
6. Have the same students switch partners and repeat steps 2 to 4.
7. After each pair completes their elevator rides, give that pair about a minute to reflect on how they shared their vision and what they learned from their feedback.
8. Repeat steps 2 to 4 and 6 with new pairs until all students have heard each other's vision. If you have a large group, repeat enough times for students to share and hear and provide and receive feedback on several visions (i.e., eight to ten).

Reflection and Connection to the Model

Remember that leadership requires deliberate practice, and creating a vision is part of that. If you think back to all the great speeches you have heard, not one of them was done without a lot of practice. A vision starts with a spark of an idea that is compelling and inviting to others. As you recall how people tried to engage you, think about how you will engage others, and quickly. We rarely have more than 60 seconds to get someone's attention.

Questions to Discuss with Those Who Provided Feedback

- What did you think when you heard your partner's vision?
- Was your partner effective in inviting you to want to share the vision with him or her?
- What feedback did or could you give that would be helpful? Identify one thing your partner could say in addition to or instead of the words he or she chose.
- Was there a specific vision that you heard today in all of the elevator speeches that resonated with you? If so, which was it, and why?

Questions to Discuss with Those Who Shared Their Visions

- Was it difficult to convey your vision with conviction and passion in 45 seconds? If so, did it get easier with each practice session?
- What skills did you use to effectively communicate your vision?
- What have you learned that will help you create a compelling elevator pitch?
- How does effective communication help you Inspire a Shared Vision?
- After receiving feedback on your vision, did you do anything differently when you expressed it in the next elevator?

Student LPI Behaviors Associated with This Activity

17 "I talk with others about how their own interests can be met by working toward a common goal."
22 "I am upbeat and positive when talking about what we can accomplish."
27 "I speak with passion about the higher purpose and meaning of what we are doing."

• • •

ACTIVITY: WORD PICTURES—ARTICULATING YOUR VISION

Submitted by Melanie Young

Objectives

Students will be able to:

- Understand the importance of being able to articulate a vision in a way that inspires their team, group, or organization to act.
- Understand the power of image in creating a shared vision

Number of Participants

- A group of any size

Time Required:

- 10 to 15 minutes

Materials and Equipment

- Paper (plain copy paper 8.5 × 11 inches works well); pencils, crayons, colored pencils, or markers
- Photo or other relatively simple picture or image (e.g., a cabin and tree); enough copies for each pair

Area Setup

- Tables and chairs set in such a way that students can face each other

Process

1. Divide the group into pairs, and have them sit facing one another at a table.
2. Give the first team member a sheet of paper and drawing instrument.
3. Give the second team member a picture. The first team member must not be able to see the picture.
4. Explain that the person with the picture is to give verbal descriptions so the other person can draw the same picture. The partner with the picture can give only verbal descriptions; nothing else (e.g., using fingers to show size) may be used. The person drawing may not ask any questions. They will have 5 minutes.
5. After 5 minutes, the pairs stop, and the person who has been drawing reveals the picture he or she has drawn.
6. When beginning the activity processing, ask the person who gave the directions to think about the parts of the drawing that surprised him or her and the person who drew to try to remember as specifically as possible what the other person said that directed him or her or what he or she was thinking that helped in deciding what to draw.
   - For those who were drawing, ask, "What about this activity was challenging?"
   - For those who were describing, ask, "What was your reaction to what your partner drew?"

- For those who were drawing, ask, "What information would have been helpful for you? If you had been able to ask questions, what questions would you have asked? What did your partner do that helped you to draw this picture? Other than more information, what could the communicator have done to help you draw the picture?"
- For those who were describing, ask, "If your partner could have asked questions, would this have helped you with the process? If so, why? What questions would have been helpful to creating a more accurate drawing?"

Variation

Repeat this activity with a different picture, this time applying some of the lessons learned from the first round to help students build their skills.

Reflection and Connection to the Model

Visions and values are concepts that are interpreted individually in much the same way that individuals interpret an image. In order to Inspire a Shared Vision, leaders must find ways to understand how people are receiving the words they say. This will inform the shared vision.

Questions to Discuss

- How can leaders ensure their team members understand and connect with the vision? Describe how leaders use word pictures, analogies, metaphors, and other symbolic language to make visions come alive.
- What happens to teams that are not clear on the vision?
- How does asking questions of others contribute to clarifying one's vision? Is there a time when asking questions can make defining a vision difficult? If so, when and how?

Student LPI Behaviors Associated with This Activity

2 "I look ahead and communicate what I believe will affect us in the future."

7 "I describe to others in our organization what we should be capable of accomplishing."

17 "I talk with others about how their own interests can be met by working toward a common goal."

ACTIVITY: GIVING LIFE TO YOUR VISION BY REFRAMING FROM WHAT TO WHY

Submitted by R. T. Good

Objectives

Students will be able to:

- Adapt their reference from the "what" of a vision to the "why" of a vision
- Understand the reframing concept
- Apply examples of framing shift to their own potential roles as leaders
- Experience reframing the concept within their own leadership contexts

Number of Participants

- Works with any size group

Time Required

- 45 minutes total
  - 20 minutes of video viewing
  - 2 minutes confirmation discussion and facilitation after viewing the video
  - 5 minutes to set up the activity and allow individual reflection
  - 8 minutes to pair and share (4 minutes each)
  - 10 minutes to debrief

Materials and Equipment

- Computer, Internet connection, and video projection with sound
- Simon Sinek video: *How Great Leaders Inspire Action*, available at http://www.youtube.com/watch?v=qp0HIF3SfI4. Sinek shares how leaders inspire action through the use of the question, "Why?" Approximately 18 minutes 30 seconds.
- Personal Reflection worksheet for each student

Area Setup

- Any setting suitable for video screening and working in discussion pairs

Facilitator Cue: Appropriate after reviewing the ideas of Inspire a Shared Vision and specifically the second commitment of Enlisting Others.

Process

1. Set up the video for display.
2. Highlight that you give life to a vision when you infuse it with powerful language using metaphors, stories, pictures, illustrations, and examples. Acknowledge that a frequent stumbling block is identifying something powerful that will move not the intellect of potential followers but their emotion, the mechanism whereby people make commitments. Getting in touch with emotion is through the why of the vision, not the what.

Facilitator Cue: This activity builds on lessons learned in the prior activity, Word Pictures: Articulating Your Vision.

3. View the video.
4. After viewing the video, hold a group discussion. Ask for examples shared in the video for the difference between a what and a why of a vision to confirm or facilitate students' understanding of the concept.
5. Distribute the worksheet, explaining that it is for the students' reference and note taking only and will not be collected.
6. Ask students to reflect on their own capacity as a leader in a current particular context—residence halls, club, sports team, work, community service, or something else, whether formal or informal—one in which they are hopeful of making a difference in how things are currently situated. Ask students to articulate the what of their vision for how things could be different, making notes on the worksheet. Then ask that they take their what and reframe it as a why: articulating the compelling and powerful why the vision they have matters and how this could be conveyed to others. Allow a few minutes for quiet reflection.
7. Ask students to form pairs to share their case for why and what in their own potential leadership capacity. After a few minutes, remind the group to switch to the other person if they have not already done so.
8. Conclude the activity by inviting several people to share their examples. You may wish to share an example of your own for how reframing helped in your capacity to be a more effective leader. This may be helpful to get the discussion started or as a conclusion to the activity. The idea is to draw out the capacity of how addressing the why of

an idea creates emotional buy-in for the what of an idea and helps with the practice of Inspiring a Shared Vision by Enlisting Others.

Reflection and Connection to the Mode

Making a vision compelling to others requires being able to answer the question of "why?" "Why" addresses issues of values much more than "what?" does. In order to create a shared vision, leaders must also understand the values of others and the aspirations they share as a group. This exercise helps develop the skill of being able to tap into what really matters to people, why they care, and creating the potential to make meaningful connections and a shared sense of future possibilities.

Student LPI Behaviors Associated with This Activity

2 "I look ahead and communicate what I believe will affect us in the future."
7 "I describe to others in our organization what we should be capable of accomplishing."
12 "I talk with others about a vision of how things could be even better in the future."
17 "I talk with others about how their own interests can be met by working toward a common goal."
22 "I am upbeat and positive when talking about what we can accomplish."
27 "I speak with passion about the higher purpose and meaning of what we are doing."

STUDENT WORKSHEET: PERSONAL REFLECTION—GIVING LIFE TO YOUR VISION BY REFRAMING FROM WHAT TO WHY

Part 1

Think of a context in which you have the capacity to be a leader (formal or informal is unimportant); it could be with a classroom assignment, in the residence halls, a community service project, or a campus club, organization, or team, or possibly off-campus (e.g., at work, church, volunteer group). Name that context:

Envision something that you think is important in that context that could be changed for the better and that requires others to help make it a reality. Identify it and describe your proposed change:

Identify *why* making that change matters. Why is the difference it will make an important one? Try to bring your reason alive through story, metaphor, pictures, illustrations, or some other device to help it take on life. Describe why the change will have a real impact:

Part 2

Find another participant in the room with whom to partner and share your idea. In speaking with your partner, imagine that she or he is someone from whom you need support in order to achieve your vision. However, *and this is important*, share your idea backward. Don't start with the what of the idea; try not to even disclose the what until near the end if possible. Start with the why that drives you toward the what. Provide for your partner a thorough understanding of why you are compelled into action and why supporting this endeavor is important. Then ask for his or her support to do what you seek to do!

ACTIVITY: VISUALIZE YOURSELF

Submitted by Vanessa Schoenherr

Objectives

Students will be able to:

- Create a clear and purposeful vision
- Describe and share that vision

Number of Participants

- Ideal for 20 to 30 people gathered in one location

Time Required

- 5 to 20 minutes depending on the number of participants

Materials and Equipment:

- Writing implements and paper (plain copier paper 8.5 × 11 inches works well) for each participant

Area Setup

- Chairs in a circle so that for the later part of the activity, participants can see and engage with each other freely
- A location that should allow participants to feel relaxed and be comfortable

Facilitator Cue: This activity focuses specifically on the first commitment of Inspire a Shared Vision: Envision the Future.

Process

1. Tell students this is a visualization activity, so they should get comfortable in their seats; when they are, they should close their eyes. Let them know that they will remain here with their eyes closed for the entire exercise and no one will touch them, so they should feel safe and relaxed.

2. Ask them to take a few deep breaths, exhaling through their mouth.
3. When they are quiet, say:

   We will now go on a journey into the future.

   Think of a something you hope to accomplish or a dream you have. This can be a personal aspiration like completing a marathon or a professional one like starting your own company. Even if this isn't something you are pursuing right now, you can still envision this aspiration or dream because it's important to you.

   Now the day has come, and you have turned your dream into reality. Think about the surroundings on this day. What's going on? (pause) What are you saying and doing? (pause) Who else is there? (pause) What do your surroundings look like? (pause) How do you feel?

   Keep these images clear in your mind, and begin to slowly rewind back to where you are right now.

   Chances are your journey had stops along the way. What were they? Were the stops positive or negative experiences? Was the trip smooth and uneventful, or bumpy and turbulent? What obstacles did you encounter? How did you work through these obstacles? Did you have to sacrifice anything to get where you are? What was that sacrifice? Consider the time it took to get through each one? Were you persistent? What did you learn about yourself?

   Now open your eyes.

4. Now say, "On the blank sheet of paper, quickly write about or draw pictures of some of the things you saw. This can be descriptive words or specific images. Work quickly." Give them two minutes and then ask, "Who needs more time?" If anyone does, tell them they have 1 more minute.

Facilitator Cue: If time permits, ask students to share their vision with others in a small group. The feedback they receive can help identify logical steps to realize that vision and make it feel achievable. If you say, for example, "I saw myself with a large group of friends and they were looking to me for guidance," someone in the group might respond, "I can see you being president of your sorority [or fraternity]. You're already doing some of the things you'll need to learn about."

You can also make a handout with the questions listed above to do as a homework assignment. Filling in the details takes time, but this effort can open students' thinking about next steps.

Reflection and Connection to the Model

A compelling vision of the future starts from within. This exercise help develop students' skill of being able to tap into what really matters to them, creating the potential to make meaningful connections and a clear sense of future possibilities.

Student LPI Behaviors Associated with This Activity

Although this activity applies to a personal vision, it is a great starting point and demonstrates the behaviors below if you change *I* to *we.* It creates the deliberate practice that can then be translated to visioning for "we."

17 "I talk with others about how their own interests can be met by working toward a common goal."

22 "I am upbeat and positive when talking about what we can accomplish."

27 "I speak with passion about the higher purpose and meaning of what we are doing."

• • •

ACTIVITY: SNAPSHOTS OF SUCCESS

Submitted by Katie Burke

Objectives

Students will be able to:

- Understand what it means to Inspire a Shared Vision
- Consider how their visions are perceived by others and how to better articulate their cause

Number of Participants

- 5 to 50 participants

Time Required

- 30 to 45 minutes

Adapted from "What Does Success Look Like?" submitted by Amanda Itliong for J. M. Kouzes, Barry Z. Posner, and E. Beich, *The Leadership Challenge Activities Book* (San Francisco: Jossey-Bass/Pfeiffer, 2010).

Materials and Equipment

- One sheet of plain white paper for each participant (copier paper 8.5 × 11 inches works well)
- Colored markers, pencils, or crayons
- Pen or pencil for each participant
- Sticky putty or tape to hang drawings on the wall
- Five to ten sticky notes for each participant

Area Setup

- Table space for participants
- Wall space for hanging drawings and comments

Facilitator Cue: This activity should be done before in-depth teaching on the practice of Inspire a Shared Vision. The activity assists students in understanding how to apply the practice and the importance of communicating it effectively to their peers. The facilitator should be conscious of students' focusing too much on the drawing of their snapshot picture instead of the clear communication of a moment in a successful project. Feel free to leave the showcase up as long as you'd like after the activity.

Process

1. Have students seated at tables.
2. Give each student one blank sheet of paper, plus colored markers, pencils, or crayons.
3. Ask students to imagine a project that they have just started working on or are about to start. Urge them to think about the end product and what it looks like when it is determined a success.
4. After a moment or two, ask the students to now imagine that they have taken a snapshot of the most successful moment of that project. Tell them to think about what and who is in the picture (at least one person should be in it). Ask them what actions the people involved are taking and what they are saying or feeling. Also ask them to identify when and where the project is taking place.
5. Give students about 5 minutes to draw the snapshot they imagined, leaving the bottom third of the paper blank. Remind them that their artistic capabilities do not matter in this exercise; for example, they can simply draw stick figures and label them. This is just a different approach to help them explore their visions.

6. Give the students 3 to 5 minutes to write commentary on the bottom third of the paper—mainly the who, what, where, when, and how. Remind students to write neatly so that other people can easily read what they described.
7. Ask the participants to hang their vision pictures in the part of the room given to their pictures, subbed the "Showcase of Visions." This will be the showcase of their vision pictures.
8. For the next 5 to 10 minutes, depending on the size of the group, have all the participants visit the showcase and think about two questions: (1) "What did you see in the other participants' snapshots that drew you in, that made the vision effective? Or was there was something that distracted you, making the snapshots less effective?" (2) "What did you see in the other participants' snapshots that you want to include in your own vision?"
9. Direct students to leave a comment (using the sticky notes) for the other participants relating to the effectiveness of the vision or any other feedback they'd like to share.
10. Debrief with students by reminding them they do not need to actually show the drawing to anyone, but they should focus on how people are contributing and what the reactions are, both verbal and nonverbal, once that successful end has been met. This can help all the members feel more connected to the visions and more likely to work to see it through to the end.

Variations

- If you have a group that happens to be working on a project together, ask them to get into small groups and share their insights about what success might look like on their project based on these drawings and comments. What can they do moving forward to make these visions a reality?
- Because most students are likely to have a mobile phone with a camera and photo album, instead of drawing a picture of the future, they could take a photo of something that represents their ideal future in response to instructions 3 and 4 above. Or they could select an image from their album that represents the future they desire. This could then be used in the paired discussions.

Reflection and Connection to the Model

It takes time for leaders craft a vision. It starts with a spark of an idea, but that spark must start a flame in more than just the leader. Getting feedback on your vision and looking at what others have done that inspires you is an effective way to shape the vision so that others may connect with it and move it toward becoming a shared vision.

Student LPI Behaviors Associated with This Activity

17 "I talk with others about how their own interests can be met by working toward a common goal."
22 "I am upbeat and positive when talking about what we can accomplish."
27 "I speak with passion about the higher purpose and meaning of what we are doing."

• • •

ACTIVITY: VISION, VALUES, AND ROCK AND ROLL

Submitted by Andrew Moyer

Objectives:

Students will be able to:

- Explore the impact that music has on their motivation
- Comprehend how language can be used to build a common vision
- Identify wording that clarifies their vision

Number of Participants

- No more than 10

Time Required

- 45 to 60 minutes

Materials and Equipment

- Internet connection
- Computer with speakers
- iPod/MP3 player and docking station or a CD player, or perhaps both

Facilitator Cue: Have students read the chapters on Inspire a Shared Vision in *The Student Leadership Challenge* prior to doing the exercise.

Facilitator Cue: The materials you use will depend on how you have students share the song they have chosen. Choose the format that is simplest for your session. This could be a CD with all of the songs already on it or using YouTube to play the songs.

Area Setup

- A room that is secluded or can be closed off and arranged so that all participants can hear the music

Facilitator Cue: This activity challenges students to think of a song that has had an impact on them. There are songs that are embedded in our culture as songs that Inspire a Shared Vision. A few examples are "Imagine" by John Lennon, "What a Wonderful World" by Louis Armstrong, and "If You're Out There" by John Legend." These songs serve as a call to action and paint a clear image of the actions the singers hoped people would take. Students should pick a song that conveys an image of the ways things can be.

Process

1. Before the session in which you use this activity, give students this assignment:

    Select a song that inspires you or has inspired you in the past. It can be any song that you feel depicts a clear and compelling vision. Then think about the words the artist uses and how they contribute to the power of the song. Bring copies of the lyrics for our next session. We will be using [insert the format you will use] for playing the song. Bring enough copies for each participant.

2. For the session with the activity, have the students pass out the copies of their song's lyrics to share when they play the song for the group. Have each student play his or her song and ask the others what they heard in it that resonated for them personally.
3. Once everyone has had a turn sharing his or her song and lyrics and hearing responses, discuss the connection between this experience and Inspire a Shared Vision. What did these songs accomplish in terms of vision, values, and community?

Reflection and Connection to the Model

A compelling vision of the future starts with the values we hold. In order to create a shared vision, leaders must understand the values of others and the aspirations they share as a group. Many of the lyrics will also convey the power of using metaphors and analogies to help people see the same things. This exercise helps develop the skill of being able to tap into what really matters to people, creating the potential to make meaningful connections and a shared sense of future possibilities.

Questions to Discuss

- How does language affect what you mean when you share your vision and what others think when they hear your vision?
- How can you apply the feeling that you hear, read, or see in music (and even other arts, literature, or other expressive forms) to how you express a vision to others?
- What does crafting a vision in a way that others may imagine the future do for clarifying your vision and helping others understand the vision better?

Student LPI Behaviors Associated with This Activity

2 "I look ahead and communicate what I believe will affect us in the future."
7 "I describe to others in our organization what we should be capable of accomplishing."
12 "I talk with others about a vision of how things could be even better in the future."
17 "I talk with others about how their own interests can be met by working toward a common goal."
22 "I am upbeat and positive when talking about what we can accomplish."
27 "I speak with passion about the higher purpose and meaning of what we are doing."

• • •

ACTIVITY: SUM IT ALL UP

Submitted by Beth High

Objectives

Students will be able to:

- Understand how connecting a symbol to a vision makes it accessible to people after the formal presentation
- Identify a symbol (a song, an image, an object, a phrase) they can use with a vision they have about something they think can be better for others in the future

Number of Participants

- Any size group

Time Required

- 30 to 45 minutes

Materials and Equipment

- Plain paper 8.5 × 11 inches for each participant
- Writing tool for each participant

Area Setup

- A hard surface for students to draw on: at tables, desks, in a lecture hall, or even sitting on the floor

Facilitator Cue: This activity challenges students to use the right side of their brain. You may find students resistant to drawing, thinking they "can't draw." Let them know they will be describing what they drew, so anything goes.

Process

1. Ask students to think about a situation in their life right now that is "broken." This might be the way people are working together, lack of information, lack of resources, the way resources are accessed, and so on.

Facilitator Cue: Encourage them to pick something they believe can be fixed. Not only do they believe it, but they have a clear idea of what things would be like if they were fixed.

2. Have students draw a vertical line down the center of the paper. On the left side, they are to draw a picture of the problem; on the right side, what it looks like fixed.

Facilitator Cue: Don't let the students get too bogged down in the drawing. Inform them that an image or an idea will float up into their thinking. Grab it and draw. You can also help them with this cue: "This situation is like the . . . And the remedy is like a . . . "

3. Once everyone has had a chance to draw on both sides of the page (usually about 10 minutes) have everyone get into small groups and describe what they drew.

Facilitator Cue: People are inclined to dive into the situation, so guide them to give the person feedback on the solution side only.

Facilitator Cue: If time permits have the groups select one or two of their favorites to present to the larger group. Facilitate a conversation about what was compelling about the drawing. Why did they choose it?

4. Help students understand that the drawing can quickly and effectively capture all the things they discussed when they described the problem and the solution to their groups. Finding a way to sum the ideas can help a leader carry the vision forward to other situations.
5. Ask students if they can think of a way to capture the ideas even more efficiently by identifying a symbol for the solution. A symbol is something like a red cross (representing medical aid) or a graphic fork and knife (indicating restaurant locations). Ask students to think about an object, a shape, a sign, letter, or other image that symbolizes the solution, or if there is a symbol they can pull from the drawing

Reflection and Connection to the Model

Finding a symbol for your vision makes it possible to carry it forward and to have those you lead hold it when you are not around. What kind of symbols can you identify that have done this? This exercise help develop the skill of being able to tap into what really matters to people, creating the potential to make meaningful connections and a shared sense of future possibilities.

Student LPI Behaviors Associated with This Activity

2 "I look ahead and communicate what I believe will affect us in the future."
7 "I describe to others in our organization what we should be capable of accomplishing."
12 "I talk with others about a vision of how things could be even better in the future."
17 "I talk with others about how their own interests can be met by working toward a common goal."
22 "I am upbeat and positive when talking about what we can accomplish."
27 "I speak with passion about the higher purpose and meaning of what we are doing."

ACTIVITY: FINISH THE STORY

Submitted by Larry Mannolini III

Objectives

Students will be able to:

- Create an atmosphere within their organization that encourages vision
- Gain an appreciation for the capacity within each member of a group to have their own vision of the future
- Explore the concept of a shared vision and the importance of seeking input from others

Number of Participants

- Small groups of no more than 8 students each

Time Required

- 35 to 45 minutes

Facilitator Cue: This activity can be adapted for use by student organizations made up of larger numbers of students or with smaller groups such as their executive boards. This activity can be conducted within an organization (e.g., in the planning stages of their year) or in a workshop of a large group of people. You will need to monitor time. Let participants know how much time they have to complete each task.

Materials and Equipment

- Flip chart paper for each group
- Marker, pen, or pencil for each student
- A copy of the Finish the Story worksheet and extra lined paper for each student

Facilitator Cue: Students should have read the chapters on Inspire a Shared Vision in *The Student Leadership Challenge.*

Area Setup

- A large open space area, with round tables that seat at least 8 students at each
- Enough room between the tables so that students cannot easily hear those at nearby tables talking

Process

1. Prior to the activity, write a sample story that sets up a moment in the future where there has been some kind of meaningful success. Base the story on the audience type (students from a defined organization, such as resident assistants or members of the same sorority, or students from different types of groups). An alternative is to use this story:

   > It is the end of the year, and you are at the annual Leadership and Service Awards banquet celebrating the achievements of individuals and organizations from the past year. You are the president of the organization that won Student Organization of the Year. You are excited and proud of the award your group has just won as you walk up to the stage and accept your award. The award presenter directs you to the podium to say a few words about the award and what your group did to deserve it. You begin by saying:

2. Copy the story you will be using in the "Story" section on the Finish the Story worksheet prior to copying the form for the participants.
3. Have participants form groups of no more than eight people, and have them sit together at a table. If this exercise is being done in a single organization, splitting up in groups may not be necessary.
4. Pass out a copy of the Finish the Story worksheet and a writing instrument to each student.
5. Have each student complete the story on the worksheet. Extra lined paper can be used to complete the stories if necessary.

Facilitator Cue: Encourage students to be creative in their story writing. This is their opportunity to paint the picture of success from their unique perspective. Let them know how much time they have to do this.

6. When everyone at a table has finished the story, each student in turn reads the entire story to the group and explains why he or she chose to end it in that way and believes that his or her vision could be realized. Students should be as specific and detailed as possible in this part of the activity.

7. Each group makes a list of common themes in the various stories. A recorder should be assigned to collect common themes of change and vision on the flip chart paper using the markers.
8. After all the stories have been shared and common themes identified and captured, each group selects a member to share their common vision themes (as recorded on the flip chart paper) with the larger audience.
9. Throughout the group sharing exercise, the facilitator should emphasize the key points and importance of enlisting others in a shared vision.
10. Following the activity, the facilitator collects all the flip chart paper, consolidates the results, and distributes them to all students or the group (whichever is appropriate).

Facilitator Cue: It is through sharing each person's story ending that the participants can see each one. The idea behind this exercise is to provide an opportunity for participants to write the ending of a story that will, by writing it as a group, incorporate each person's vision of the organization's future. The facilitator can either utilize the sample story from the Finish the Story Worksheet, or make up his or her own based on the unique circumstances of the group in question. The basic idea is to start the story and let the participants write the ending.

Reflection and Connection to the Model

This practice is called Inspire a *Shared* Vision because it is not enough for an individual member to have a clear vision of the future of the organization. It needs to be a shared vision, and the only way that comes about is by listening to the hopes and aspirations of others. A common vision that effectively steers the actions of an organization emerges when each member finds that vision compelling. By starting with a clear understanding of what each individual member sees as success, a group has a better opportunity to appeal to all its members with a shared vision of success.

Student LPI Behaviors Associated with This Activity

2 "I look ahead and communicate what I believe will affect us in the future."
7 "I describe to others in our organization what we should be capable of accomplishing."
12 "I talk about a vision of how things could be even better in the future."
17 "I talk with others about how their own interests can be met by working toward a common goal."

22 "I am upbeat and positive when talking about what we can accomplish."
27 "I speak with passion about the higher purpose and meaning of what we are doing."

Application to Other Practices

Replace the first part of the story on the Finish the Story worksheet with a challenge the group is facing and have each participant offer suggestions of ways to face or overcome it. This application supports Challenge the Process: participants look beyond their own experience and also create an environment where it is safe to think openly and creatively about how to resolve issues, both core to Challenge the Process.

STUDENT WORKSHEET: FINISH THE STORY

Name:

This exercise provides an opportunity for you to write the ending to a story that will incorporate your vision about the organization's future.

Instructions: Write the ending to the story that follows. Stories should be forward thinking and incorporate an ideal vision of the best outcome you'd like to see. Be creative, and don't be afraid to take risks in your vision! When everyone in your group has finished, each of you will share your story with the rest of the group.

Story

Read this partial story and supply your own ending. Use additional paper if necessary:

It is the end of the year, and you are sitting at the annual Leadership and Service Awards banquet celebrating the achievements of both individuals and organizations from the past year. You are the president of the organization that won Student Organization of the Year. You are excited and proud of the award your group has just won as you walk up to the stage and accept your award. The award presenter directs you to the podium to say a few words about the award and what your group did to deserve it. You begin by saying:

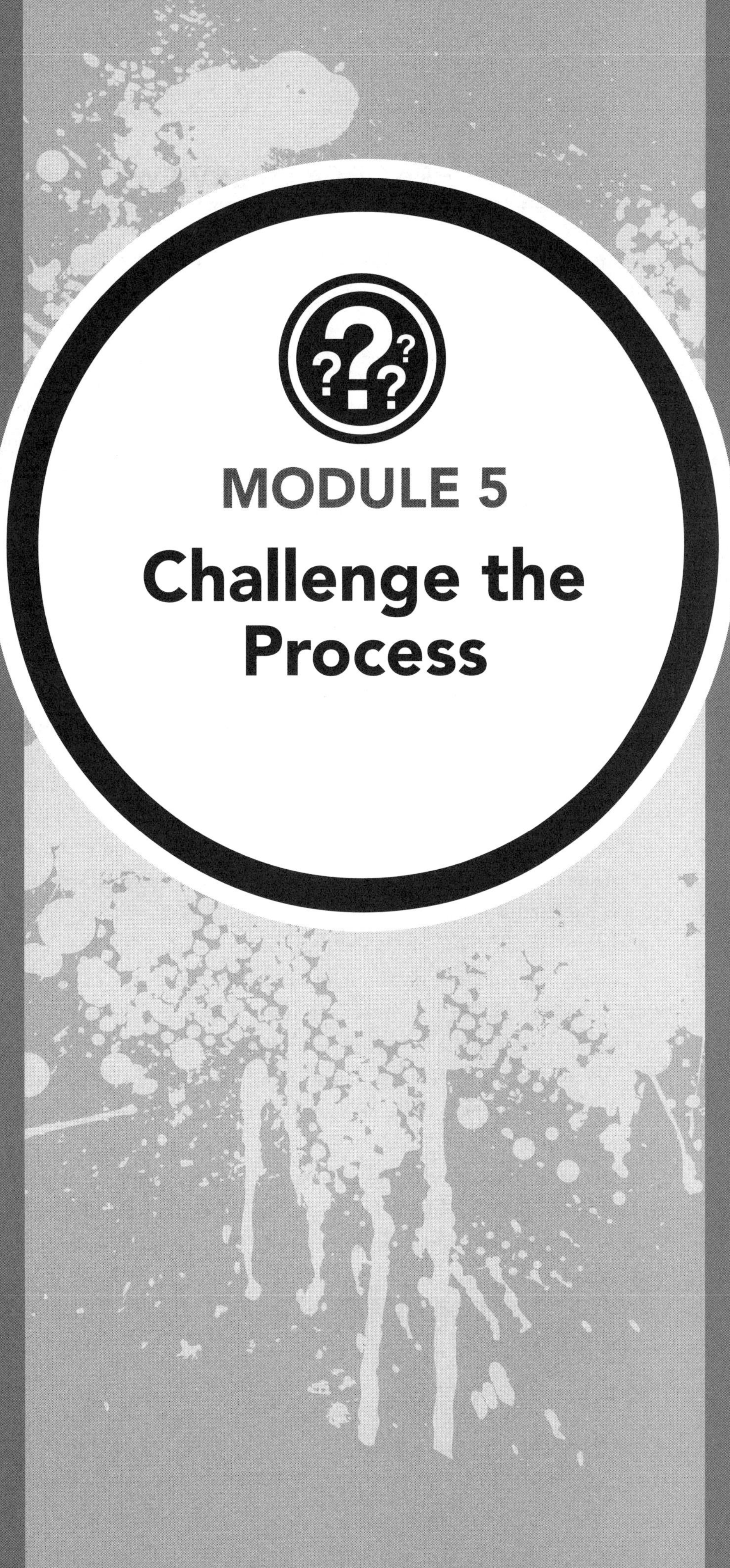

MODULE 5
Challenge the Process

PRACTICE OVERVIEW

Challenge the Process: Search for Opportunities and Experiment and Take Risks

Leaders search for opportunities by seizing the initiative and looking outward for innovative ways to improve. They experiment and take risks by constantly generating small wins and learning from experience.

Leaders are pioneers. They are willing to step out into the unknown. The work of leaders is change, and the status quo is unacceptable to them. They search for opportunities to innovate, grow, and improve. In doing so, they experiment and take risks. Because leaders know that risk-taking involves mistakes and failures, they accept the inevitable disappointments as learning opportunities. Leaders constantly ask, "What can we learn when things don't go as planned?"

WHY STUDENTS SHOULD CHALLENGE THE PROCESS

Leaders create visions, and visions are about the future. What leaders imagine does not yet exist. To move forward into the unknown requires them to do things differently. If they don't Challenge the Process, things will likely stay the same, and eventually get worse. Challenging the Process means taking initiative and the incremental steps to begin transforming possibilities into realities.

Students who have completed the Personal-Best Leadership Experience, an exercise that captures and explores a successful leadership experience in one's past, know that the pride they felt in association with that experience is rooted in the fact that it was not an easy task. Stepping into the unknown is difficult but necessary in order to create change. The more comfortable students become with this idea, the more likely they are to try it out. The activities in this module help reinforce for them the need to change to achieve great things.

Challenge the Process isn't about change for the sake of change. It's about questioning the status quo with the intention of making things better. The work of student leaders is to change for the greater good, not for personal gain. These activities are designed to reinforce this concept.

Activities List

- House of Cards
- "Orientation: The Time of Your Life"—A Skit
- Going, Going, Gone
- This is How We've Always Done It . . . But Let's Try Something Else

- Turning Big Challenges into Incremental Action Steps
- Brick Walls Don't Have to Stop You
- Planning with the End in Mind
- The Six Thinking Hats

• • •

ACTIVITY: HOUSE OF CARDS

Submitted by Reba Noel

Objectives

Students will be able to:

- Explore thinking beyond the status quo
- Recognize the value of innovative thinking when presented with a challenge
- See the value of outsight—the act of looking for new information and insight from external sources when exploring ways to improve a project

Number of Participants

- Any size group

Time Required

- 30 minutes or more

Materials and Equipment

- 1 full deck of playing cards (52 cards per deck) for every 3 participants

Area Setup

- Any space with a number of flat, level, smooth surfaces (e.g., tables)

Facilitator Cue: Before starting an instructional module on Challenge the Process, have participants do this activity to introduce them to the importance of innovative thinking. Once you have completed the activity, introduce the module and tie the behaviors to the process that participants encountered when doing this activity.

Process

1. Have participants form groups of three and situate themselves at a table or other flat surface.
2. Hand each group a deck of playing cards.
3. Explain to the groups they will be given a number of challenges that they will use their deck of cards to attempt to complete. Explain to the groups that a point system will be used in evaluating each group's work. The group with the most points at the end of the activity will win a prize—perhaps a candy bar for each member of the group. (You may also opt not to give a prize.)
4. Present the following challenges, in order, to the groups:

Facilitator Cue: This exercise encourages creative and innovative thought as participants strive to build a house that is functional, meets the challenge put forward, and is competitive.

- *Challenge 1:* Tell the groups, "You have 10 minutes to build a freestanding house of cards that is as structurally sound as you can make it (i.e., one that can stand up on its own), using all of the cards in your deck (and no other materials except for the cards)." Once the groups have finished, ask them to describe what commonalities they notice in the various group efforts.

Facilitator Cue: Most people when told to construct a house of cards automatically start to build a pyramid shape. See if there are any other shapes. Give 1 point for a construction that is not in a pyramid shape. If your groups construct a certain type of common structure, you may choose to award points for alternate types of structures.

- *Challenge 2:* Have the groups remove cards, one at a time, from their construction. Give 1 point for each card removed. Once the groups have finished, ask each one what happens when a card is (or cards are) removed. Is the result what they expected? If the result met their expectations, ask why they designed a construction that had a *known* fault? Discuss what conversations they had and what choices they made that resulted in a flawed outcome.
- *Challenge 3:* Start over by having each group build another house of cards with height as a consideration. Encourage them to keep in mind the issues they faced and the choices they made in the previous challenge. Give 1 point for each level or story of their construction. Once the groups have finished, ask what new challenges they faced in constructing this house with a different

priority. What did the groups do that was similar to or different from the first construction?

5. The group with the most points wins a prize.

Reflection and Connection to the Model

Challenge the Process begins with your own thinking. Leaders find ways to open the windows to their thinking, letting new ideas float in and perhaps old ideas to float out. When leaders demonstrate their capacity to explore new ideas and perspectives, they are modeling that behavior for those they hope to engage in the same kind of thinking.

Questions to Discuss

- What can be learned from an "if it's not broke, don't fix it" attitude?
- How did this activity encourage innovative thought?
- Did all members in a group have a chance to try out their ideas? What options were suggested in your group that you didn't try? Why?
- What processes or considerations did you take into account when addressing the final challenge (building for height versus strength)?
- Were there any lessons learned from the first challenge that helped you with the final challenge?
- Did you notice any other leadership exhibited in this activity?

Student LPI Behaviors Associated with This Activity

8 "I look for ways that others can try out new ideas and methods."
13 "I search for innovative ways to improve what we are doing."
18 "When things don't go as expected, I ask, 'What can we learn from this experience?'"
28 "I take initiative in experimenting with the way things can be done."

• • •

ACTIVITY: "ORIENTATION: THE TIME OF YOUR LIFE"—A SKIT

Submitted by Cliff Raphael

Objectives

Students will be able to:

- Recap the key concepts of Challenge the Process through a dramatization
- Consolidate the key concepts of Challenge the Process

Number of Participants

- Any size group

Time Required:

- 5 to 15 minutes to rehearse the skit
- 15 minutes to present the skit

Materials and Equipment

- 6 copies of the script for the skit (suggested script provided)
- A large three-ring binder (or notebook of some sort) completely filled with papers (any type of scrap papers or notes) to use as a prop for the skit

Area Setup

- Table and 5 chairs centrally placed
- Chairs or desks for the rest of the group arranged in a semicircle or U-shape.

Facilitator Cue: This activity is to be done after students have learned the Challenge the Process content by reading the appropriate chapters in *The Student Leadership Challenge* or covering it in a class or workshop.

Process

1. Choose (or ask for volunteers) six students to present the skit (five actors plus one stage manager/director).
2. Provide each of these six students with a copy of the script for the skit. Allow them 5 to 10 minutes for rehearsal and other preparation. Tell the actors that although they have a script, some ad-libbing is allowed.
3. During rehearsal, the rest of the class reviews Challenge the Process content.
4. When the actors are ready, the director announces the start of the skit—for example: "The six Fs present 'Orientation: The Time of Your Life.'"
5. Ask the audience to look for specific examples of Challenge the Process concepts as the skit unfolds.
6. The director announces the end of the skit.

Reflection and Connection to the Model

Challenge the Process is about thinking in new ways and seeking new approaches to addressing problems or challenges. It is also about helping others feel safe to experiment and take risks so they can explore what might work to achieve success. Leaders create a learning environment where people feel free to experiment and learn from their experience. This activity helps explore how different people may act when faced with an opportunity to Challenge the Process and as a result better understand their own thinking about the practice. Use some or all of the questions here to encourage your students to recap the key concepts of Challenge the Process.

Begin a conversation with the actors to have them share their experience in developing, rehearsing, and performing in the skit as their specific character.

- Actors, were you comfortable in the role you played? Why? Why not?

Continue the conversation with the entire group:

- Which character did you most identify with? Why?
- Why do you think Fred was initially resistant to the prospect of changing things? What did you see and hear that led you to think that?
- What did you notice about how the new ideas were introduced? How were they accepted or rejected?
- Have you ever experienced anything different when you've introduced a new idea to a group? What did you experience, and how did you (and others) react?
- Do you think it was a helpful way to introduce new ideas? Why? Why not? What would you do differently?
- Describe the elements or concepts of Challenge the Process (i.e., the behaviors) that you saw demonstrated in the skit.
- Where did you see behaviors that were not representative of Challenge the Process?
- As leaders, what value do you see for the group or the outcome when you Challenge the Process?

Student LPI Behaviors Associated with This Activity

3 "I look for ways to develop and challenge my skills and abilities."
8 "I look for ways that others can try out new ideas and methods."
13 "I search for innovative ways to improve what we are doing."
23 "I make sure that big projects we undertake are broken down into smaller and doable portions."
28 "I take initiative in experimenting with the way things can be done."

Application to Other Practices

Student leaders could be divided into teams and asked to create skits to illustrate key concepts for each of the five practices.

If you create an alternative skit, you could build into the script other specific behaviors of any of The Five Practices of Exemplary Leadership. If you allow the actors to create their own skits, you could ask reflection questions about any of the other practices that were demonstrated. If other leadership behaviors were not demonstrated, talk about what things a person in the scenario could do that would exhibit more apparent leadership behavior.

SUGGESTED SCRIPT: "ORIENTATION: THE TIME OF YOUR LIFE"

Frances (director/stage manager): announces: The six Fs [Frank, Fred, Francine, Fiona, Finlay, and Frances] present: "Orientation: The Time of Your Life (Reprising Challenge the Process)"

(Student government members enter the room and sit at table)

Frank: Welcome to our new team members—Finley, Frances, and Fiona—to our first planning meeting. Our big project this term is to plan the student orientation activities for this fall. [Reaches for binder.] I have the binder here from the past five years of orientation activities. We can use that and make our lives easy.

Francine: I think we need to do some new and different things for this orientation because we need more student involvement. That's part of the reason that I signed up for student government. Just imagine, hundreds of students involved in a bunch of cool activities to begin their first week! That will set them up for a positive experience all term long.

Frank: That's all very well and good, but I think we need to stick with what we know works!

Fred: But if we keep on doing what we have always done, we will keep on getting what we have always gotten, and nothing will ever change or get better!

(Conversation buzz around the table.)

Fiona: What if we set up an organized chaos event? We did that at my old school.

(Conversation buzz around the new idea.)

Finlay: I think that's a good idea, and then we can have teams from every department and every program involved.

Fred: What if we set up a "minute to win it" competition? We could have the events going all week long at lunchtime with the final rounds on the Friday of orientation week. We should definitely get some interest, especially if we have good prizes.

(Conversation buzz around the group about a great idea.)

Francine: You know, we could probably get some local merchants to sponsor prizes. We could also ask the bookstore manager to help out with prizes and the communications department to help out with marketing.

Finlay: We need to write these down. I am a lousy scribe.

(Someone volunteers to be the recorder.)

Fiona: Finlay and I attended orientation at College of the North last fall, and they had some really great ideas that generated lots of participation and lots of enthusiasm. People looked as if they were really enjoying themselves. I think we should think about using some of their ideas.

(Frank, who seemed to be going along up to this point, suddenly pipes up.)

Frank (looking frustrated): Guys, this is becoming way bigger than I am comfortable with! Instead of being the time of their lives, it could be the biggest flop or failure of ours!

Fred: Frank, I agree. It is huge. What if we broke it down into smaller individual projects, like bite-size bits? That way we can score some small wins to help build the momentum.

Group: That's a great idea!

Frances: We could begin by drafting a letter we can take to potential sponsors explaining what we are doing and asking for their help. *(Buzz around the group as the scene fades out.)*

ACTIVITY: GOING, GOING, GONE

Submitted by Natalie Loeb

Objectives

Students will be able to:

- Identify, understand, and push the boundaries of what could be
- Inspire creative energy and observe the results

Number of Participants

- Ideal for groups with a minimum of 16 people; for fewer students, adjust the number of teams appropriate to the team descriptions

Time Required

- 15 to 30 minutes

Materials and Equipment

- Paper and writing tools for each team
- Flip chart paper
- Play money ($250 per table team)
- A bag filled with enough random items for four per group plus a half-dozen extras

Facilitator Cue: Each group will pick at least four items from the bag as described below.

Area Setup

- A table for each team
- A podium or table at the front of the room for teams demonstrating their wares

Facilitator Cue: This activity is effective prior to teaching on Challenge the Process and after. If you decide to do this activity prior to teaching the practice, you might use or adapt the following text to encourage thinking about the behaviors related to Challenge the Process to see how the teams respond to its behaviors while they engage in this activity (it is common for teams to get carried away with the excitement of the activity and lose sight of the ideas behind the model).

> Challenge the Process is about pushing yourself and your group or team to the cutting edge. Leaders have the opportunity to create a climate where team members feel eager to explore new options and unconventional ways of looking at doing things. As a result, the student leader and the rest of the team can decide to seize opportunities and stay alert to identify areas of process improvement. They can take risks to try creative solutions to improve a process. Leaders are change agents. They initiate change and encourage team members to think differently, tapping into their own unrealized talent. This can result in new and creative ways to approach projects and problems in their work. Thinking differently can feel uncomfortable, even dangerous; however, leaders who push people out of their comfort zones and yield positive results create a group of folks always searching for excellence.

Process

1. Ask for nine volunteers so you can create three creative teams of three people each. The teams can be expanded in size and or number based on the number in the group.
2. Ask for someone to play the role of an auctioneer.
3. Split the remaining participants into three table teams with an equal number of participants.
4. Ask each table team to select a spokesperson to represent the team.
5. Give each table team $250 in play money (preferably in lower denominations such as $10 bills). They can use this money to bid on items.
6. Ask each of the creative teams to select four items from the bag. These items should not be shared with anyone except the members of their team.
7. Each creative team may have one turn to trade in any items they don't like and go back into the bag to replace that item.
8. Once each team has selected its items, it must bundle or package the items in a way that will make them attractive to the bidders. For example, they can tell a story about

the items to make them seem valuable, create links between items so they become more valuable, or make up information about the use of the items so they are valuable. Give the creative teams about 5 to 10 minutes to think about how to sell their items to the table teams.

9. Provide an opportunity for the table teams to view each creative team's items. Then have each creative team pitch their group of items to the bidders (all of the table teams together).
10. Allow the table teams to bid on the items. The auctioneer will lead the bidding process using a traditional auction-type process after each creative team has described its items. Typically the auctioneer collects one team's items and auctions them off in an energetic way, using the descriptions previously shared by that team. The auctioneer may start the bidding at any price (say, $10) and increase the bids by a certain amount each time. The table teams may in fact advance the bidding on their own by bidding any amount up to their allocation.
11. Once all teams have used their money or all items have been pitched, the activity is over.
12. The auctioneer counts up the money and identifies the creative team that generated the most money for its items.

Reflection and Connection to the Model

Leaders understand the value of innovative thinking. They also understand that this is something that may come more easily to some than to others and that everyone can use some help in thinking creatively.

Consider asking the following questions:

Questions for the Table Teams

- Why do you think the winning team won?
- What was it about their story or their presentation or pitch that elicited higher bids?
- What appealed or didn't appeal to the table teams?

Questions for the Creative Teams

- What was difficult about this exercise?
- How did you feel after you selected your items?
- How did you come up with your pitch or presentation?
- To what extent did everyone contribute to the pitch?
- How comfortable or uncomfortable did you feel pitching your story? Why?
- Where did you find new ideas about your items or how you would pitch your items?
- When did you feel most creative?

Questions for All

- How would you connect the experiences you had to Challenge the Process?
- In what ways did you see outsight, the act of looking for new information and insight from external sources, being used? Are there places the Creative Teams could have used outsight more effectively?
- How can the experiences in this activity directly apply to the roles you have as leaders?
- Are there any other specific practices or leadership behaviors you saw exhibited and how?

Student LPI Behaviors Associated with This Activity

8 "I look for ways that others can try out new ideas and methods."
13 "I search for innovative ways to improve what we are doing."
28 "I take initiative in experimenting with the way things can be done."

Application to Other Practices

This activity can easily be connected with other practices. For example, with Inspiring a Shared Vision, you might ask: How did some creative teams get people to see things differently than they might have first imagined? What analogies, metaphors, examples, etc. were used to help people "see" possible uses in the future for the auction items than they might have otherwise? Did the presenters use any special techniques to draw their audience into the bigger picture?

•••

ACTIVITY: THIS IS HOW WE'VE ALWAYS DONE IT . . . BUT LET'S TRY SOMETHING ELSE

Submitted by Aysen Ulupinar-Butzer

Objectives

Students will be able to:

- Think creatively
- Apply outsight to generate new ideas
- Speak up about the new ideas that they have
- Think of new ways to do things they have typically done the same way in the past
- Better express their ideas to others

Number of Participants

- Any size group

Time Required

- Two sessions of 45 minutes each, with time between sessions for students to explore new sources of ideas

Facilitator Cue: This activity is especially useful for students who are in groups that put on events.

Materials and Equipment

- Flip chart paper if the activity is done in small groups, or students can use an agenda or paper they have with them

Area Setup

- No specific setup needed; students can do this activity sitting around a table or in small groups throughout a room

Facilitator Cue: This activity provides an opportunity for students to explore the concept of outsight: looking outside their typical source to other campus groups or other campuses to generate ideas.

Process

1. Have students or groups either get into small groups (depending on the total size of your group) or have them take out paper to work independently.
2. Ask the students to pick one of their large-scale events that they do on campus and brainstorm a list of the marketing or promotion that they always do to promote the event.
3. Have students go around and share what they always do. Then have the students toss the lists aside. Now tell the students that a decision has been made to challenge the norm and the students have to think creatively and brainstorm innovative ideas or new ways to do the current ideas.

Facilitator Cue: If the students are having difficulty with not being able to think creatively, give them some personal examples of when you have thought of ways to do something differently.

4. Give the students 5 minutes or so to come up with as many new places to look for ideas as possible. Encourage them to think very freely.

Facilitator Cue: You might give them an example: "If you are members of a football team that has been doing the same warm-up routines for flexibility year after year but your team's injuries have increased over time, where might you look for new ideas on how to help the team be more flexible? Perhaps you could ask the gymnastics team or the swim team or a yoga instructor in the community. All of these are examples of turning to new sources for ideas."

5. Have students agree on a certain number of these new places to explore and give them an assignment: to bring back one new idea from this outside source for the next meeting and a budget for implementing that new idea.
6. At the next meeting, go around to each group that explored a new source and have them describe their budget and then list their ideas for promotions or marketing.

Variations

You can modify this activity with respect to budget. If you are doing small groups, you can give each group a different budget (no budget, low budget, high budget, or unlimited budget).

You can also apply this activity specifically to any other significant area or issue in which the group is involved. For example, use this activity around the issue of recruiting new members and retaining members throughout the year. You might have students think about how they can apply this to a traditional school or group event that seems to be done the same way every year. Perhaps the event is very successful, but certain aspects of it could be improved. If you can use this activity even on smaller areas within the group or with an activity the group does, students will begin to apply the behaviors of Challenge the Process more frequently.

Reflection and Connection to the Model

Leaders understand that the best way to find new ideas is to deliberately challenge the old ones. They don't insist that all the old ideas are wrong, but they ask others to challenge the ideas and themselves and explore ways to move to more productive or efficient ways to tackle a problem. Leaders understand that a dependable way to generate new ideas is to step away from the idea sources they have depended on to date. Looking at different professions, groups, or campuses can shift perspective and open the mind to new approaches that can be beneficial for the challenge at hand. This looking outside the usual sources is called outsight and is a tool leaders rely on to keep thinking and idea generation fresh.

To enable students to connect their learning to the everyday practice of Challenge the Process, consider doing the following:

- Open a discussion about how it felt to make change or to challenge the thought that "this is how we always have done it."
- Lead a discussion about what, if any, new skills or abilities students will need to develop or learn based on the new methods the group wants to apply.
- Ask the students how their idea can apply to other components of student activities and programming.
- Ask the students to use outsight by finding areas other than marketing promotion (e.g., operations, logistics, planning, evaluating) where the same kind of new thinking can be applied.

Facilitator Cue: In this same discussion, it is good to bring up (if the students don't bring it up) the idea that Challenge the Process doesn't mean debating everything they do but being willing see the other side.

Student LPI Behaviors Associated with This Activity

3 "I look for ways to develop and challenge my skills and abilities."
8 "I look for ways that others can try out new ideas and methods."
13 "I search for innovative ways to improve what we are doing."
28 "I take initiative in experimenting with the way things can be done."

Application to Other Practices

This activity could easily be adapted to the other four leadership practices by using the idea of outsight. Ask students to think of different ways than they are now doing to Model the Way, Inspire a Shared Vision, Enable Others to Act, or Encourage the Heart. How can they go outside of their experience and school "bubble" to see what others are doing and how that might be adapted to their circumstances?

• • •

ACTIVITY: TURNING BIG CHALLENGES INTO INCREMENTAL ACTION STEPS

Submitted by Jeff Hynes

Objectives

Students will be able to:

- Create appropriate strategies for solving problems
- Experience breaking down a big problem or complicated task into small steps
- Learn how using outsight helps leaders find new solutions and ways to address challenges and obstacles
- Develop an understanding of the importance of working collaboratively with group members to create positive change

Number of Participants

- Minimum of 24 students (four groups of 6 people each); group size can be adjusted, though it is preferable to have an even number of students in each group

Time Required

- 45 to 60 minutes

Materials and Equipment

- 4 flip charts with easels and enough markers for 4 groups
- A timer or watch
- 4 Case Scenario worksheets—1 per group
- 4 Challenge the Process Questions worksheets

Facilitator Cue: Students should have read the chapters on Challenge the Process in *The Student Leadership Challenge.*

Area Setup

- An open space with four round tables that will seat six students at each or the ability for students to easily move their desks into a discussion circle
- A designated front of the room where the four flip charts on easels are located with space for each group of six to discuss the outcome of the exercise

Facilitator Cue: The group of 24 is to be divided into four groups of six. Each of four groups will be presented with a case scenario for a specific task that will require Challenging the Process in order to achieve the desired outcome, explained in the Case Scenario worksheet.

Process

1. Divide the group of 24 into four working groups.
2. Explain the assignment, including the intended outcomes of participation: to consider the case scenarios they are given (the Case Scenarios worksheet) and discuss ways in which they can address the scenario. Students should be instructed to focus on how they can address or solve the bigger problem by demonstrating the behaviors of Challenge the Process. The intended outcomes are related directly to the learning objectives and to how students break larger projects into smaller steps and how they work together as a group. Groups should also respond to and discuss as a larger group the notes they took and their responses to the Challenge the Process Questions worksheet.
3. Distribute the case scenarios, one per group, and allow students 10 minutes to solve their scenario, including transferring answers to the flip chart.
4. Distribute one Challenge the Process Questions worksheet to each group, and allow the groups 5 minutes to answer the questions on the back of the worksheet or on a separate sheet of paper.
5. The individual groups make their presentations in which they discuss their action steps and answers to questions. Allow 5 to 7 minutes for discussion and classmate feedback.
6. As a full group wrap-up, at the end of the allotted time period for these two steps, each group takes a turn at the front of the room discussing its task, the action steps that the members developed in order to accomplish the task, and their brief responses to the questions. The rest of the class then can ask questions and provide feedback to the group.

Facilitator Cue: You may replace these scenarios with those relevant to your own school or organization. You can also increase or decrease the number of groups, though try to preserve the number of group members, by adding or reducing the number of scenarios.

Reflection and Connection to the Model

Challenge the Process is a difficult task. Leaders understand this and do what they can to help people take on challenges, try new things, and feel supported during the process. Leaders create small wins to help build confidence but also to pull the team together by showing incremental progress toward success. Leaders look outside their own group and their own visions, issues, and ideas to see how others have approached or succeeded in overcoming challenges and obstacles. Leaders don't necessarily need to find groups or issues that exactly match their specific challenge. Rather, in using outsight, they are on the lookout for any relevant and effective strategies that might apply to their own challenges. The questions on the handout for discussion in step 5 help to make this connection.

Student LPI Behaviors Associated with This Activity

8 "I look for ways that others can try out new ideas and methods."
13 "I search for innovative ways to improve what we are doing."
23 "I make sure that big projects we undertake are broken down into smaller and doable portions."
28 "I take initiative in experimenting with the way things can be done."

STUDENT WORKSHEET: CASE SCENARIOS

Case scenario 1: A group of students wants to start a new group on campus. This group has never existed on the campus before, and the possibility of establishing this group might be met with resistance from the student government.

Actions/Notes:

Case scenario 2: The student-athlete advisory committee would like to increase student attendance at sporting events, as well as support in general for athletics on the campus.

Actions/Notes:

Case scenario 3: The Student Government Association would like to increase student involvement in the student government and the activities that student government sponsors.

Actions/Notes:

Case scenario 4: A group of students would like to change the campus parking policy to make it more equitable.

Actions/Notes:

STUDENT WORKSHEET: CHALLENGE THE PROCESS QUESTIONS

1. What was the general initial feeling of the group about the level of difficulty when you first read about the task? Please explain your answer.

2. Did separating the task into smaller action steps help to make the task more manageable or less daunting? Please explain your answer.

3. By breaking down the task into smaller action steps, the group is able to generate small wins along the way. Identify a minimum of two small wins, but important ones nonetheless, that the group experienced as a result.

4. Where were the other places your group thought of looking or could look to learn of different ways to address the scenario? In other words, what other groups or schools could you research and talk with about how they addressed the obstacles in the scenario or similar obstacles from which you can learn a possible strategy? For example, how have other new organizations overcome objections to their forming? How did other athletic departments or student groups increase attendance and support at their events? How have others dealt with implementing new policies?

5. What did the group learn from the different perspectives or approaches that were brought to the discussion? Provide an example.

6. Provide examples from two group members about how the process of breaking down major tasks in smaller steps works in their daily lives.

ACTIVITY: BRICK WALLS DON'T HAVE TO STOP YOU

Submitted by Gary Morgan

Objectives

Students will be able to:

- Understand how leaders overcome obstacles through creativity
- Appreciate the concept of outsight and how it influences group work
- See the value of experimenting when looking for ways to improve a project
- Understand the need to persevere when dealing with difficult situations
- Learn from failure, frustration, and other things that can hold one back as a leader

Number of Participants

- Any size group

Time Required

- Approximately 11 minutes to 75 minutes for viewing the video (the options vary in length) and 30 minutes for discussion for each video

Materials and Equipment

- Computer, Internet access, and projector
- Access to videos listed on the Facilitator Instructions for the videos

Area Setup

- No special setup

Facilitator Cue: You may show any one or all three of the videos described on the Facilitator Instructions for the videos. Each illustrates various ways in which the leaders Challenge the Process.

Process

1. Select one or more of the videos described in the Facilitator Instructions and show them.
2. Use the Facilitator Instructions to guide a conversation about the videos. If you elect to use more than one video, facilitate the conversation about that video before moving onto the next one.

Facilitator Cue: You may choose additional videos to add to the list. To align with the spirit of this activity, we recommend you look for stories that exhibit leaders who are dealing with significant obstacles, demonstrate that how they address those obstacles shows their resilience, and indicate where they look to find potential solutions.

Facilitator Instructions: The Videos

Video 1: CBS News video from the television show 60 Minutes (aired November 12, 2012): "Children Helping Children." http://www.cbsnews.com/video/watch/?id=50135739n. 11 minutes, 51 seconds.

This is a story that begins when Craig Kielburger is in seventh grade. He hears of the death of a young boy in Pakistan who was murdered after he escaped childhood servitude and began speaking against it. Craig decided he wanted to do something to change the world as a result of learning about this boy and started a charity with eleven of his peers to "free the children." He knew that kids like him want to make a difference in their world and find meaning and purpose in their lives. Through his charity, Craig tried many things, and many of those didn't work. He learned many lessons as he built his charity into a $30 million organization working in forty-five countries. Along the way, Craig encountered numerous obstacles and brick walls, and each time he found a way through or around them.

Processing Question Suggestions

1. What are some of the obstacles Craig and his peers encountered? How did they address them?
   - What key ideas did Craig identify that led him on a path toward his vision?

Facilitator Cue: Craig asked himself, "Why not me?" to help others and then looked to the basic issues that might have led to child slavery, such as attacking hardship and ignorance.

2. What are some obstacles you have encountered either personally or in your group? Did you address those or avoid them?
    - If you addressed them, what did you do?
    - If you didn't address them, why?
    - How did you figure out what to try?
    - Why didn't Craig give up?
    - What causes you to give up or not give up?

Video 2: "Kyle Maynard: No Arms and No Legs Climbing Mount Kilimanjaro." http://www.youtube.com/watch?v=LuH4sK25AwE. 11 minutes, 12 seconds.

This is a story about how Kyle Maynard, who was born without arms or legs, decided at the age of twenty-five to climb the 19,431-foot peak of Kilimanjaro. A big part of doing this climb was to help show others their capabilities and their potential. In the process, Kyle shows what giving up does and how excuses keep people away from the things they want most in life.

Processing Question Suggestions

1. How can you apply Kyle's understanding that you need to know the difference between when you can push through something and when something might be really dangerous?
    - How does that question relate to how you determine the degree of risk you can take?
    - Where do you push yourself?
    - When do you find yourself giving up?
2. How does fear play into your decision making and the choices you make or do not make?
3. When you think of the obstacles you face, how do you determine whether they are obstacles you or your group have defined or true obstacles that you face from external forces?
    - How do you address each obstacle, perceived or real, as a leader?
    - What excuses do you or your group make that keep you away from your vision or what you want in life?
4. As a leader, when you address obstacles, persevere, and take risks, what are you showing and teaching others?
    - How does this teaching affect a group?

Video 3: "The Last Lecture with Randy Pausch." http://www.youtube.com/watch?v=ji5_MqicxSo. 1 hour, 16 minutes and 26 seconds (full version). A commercial classroom version DVD is available that is edited to approximately 30 minutes. Also, there is a book based on the Last Lecture video that you may want to assign as reading. Randy Pausch with Jeffrey Zaslow, *The Last Lecture* (New York: Hyperion, 2008).

Randy Pausch was a professor of computer science at Carnegie Mellon University who passed away from pancreatic cancer in 2008. About a month after his diagnosis, he delivered his "Last Lecture" to students and colleagues at Carnegie Mellon. A last lecture is a traditional speech at many colleges and universities in which faculty share their thoughts and ideas as if they were giving their very last lecture on what is most important to them. In Dr. Pausch's case, it was literally his last lecture.

Facilitator Cue: Although Randy's story is not that of a young leader, it shows how his life, at a young age and beyond, shaped his perspective on life and reveals great insights into how leaders can continually Challenge the Process, as he did not only in his current circumstances, but on how he lived his entire life.

Processing Question Suggestions (based on the full-version video)

1. Describe some things as a leader (or within your group) that you have failed at.
    - Did you do anything at the time you failed to process and talk about that experience? (If not, why didn't you?)
    - What have you learned from those failures?
    - Are there other types of learning that were valuable from such experiences (i.e., indirect learning)?
    - If others were involved, did you get feedback from them? If so, what did you learn about yourself as a leader from that feedback?
2. Thinking back on Randy's stories and experiences of facing brick walls, how do you see yourself in those situations?
    - What could you be doing differently as you face obstacles?
    - What have you done that is successful? Not successful?
3. How do your dreams for yourself or your group, or both, help you drive through obstacles?
    - How do you solve problems with others? What works? What doesn't work? Do you continue to repeat any of the actions that do not work? Why?
    - What helps you persevere? What holds you back? Why?
    - What does either of these behaviors do to others in your group?
4. As a leader, what can you do in advance to deal with the obstacles (whether you know what they are or not)?

Facilitator Cue: This is an opportunity to talk about the necessity of preparing (i.e., Randy's comments on "luck being where preparation meets opportunity"). This is also an opportunity to talk about the idea of preparation in all aspects of a student's life, from the classroom, to personally, to preparing for an internship or graduation and career (or seeking out what next steps to pursue).

Reflection and Connection to the Model

With each video, you will find evidence of leaders finding new ways to overcome obstacles and barriers of many types. The leaders shown in these videos talk about their experiences to achieve tremendous goals, live out their dreams, and create life-changing experiences for others. In each of the stories, you will see tremendous resilience and perseverance. You will find creative ways in which the storytellers created new initiatives, learned lessons through their failures, and led change because things needed to be better.

As a follow-up assignment, consider challenging students to take a lesson they viewed and learned from the video and apply it to a situation they are dealing with personally, as a leader, or as a group. Follow up at an appropriate time to have students share their experiences in applying the lessons and the outcomes that ensued.

Student LPI Behaviors Associated with This Activity

3 "I look for ways to develop and challenge my skills and abilities."
8 "I look for ways that others can try out new ideas and methods."
13 "I search for innovative ways to improve what we are doing."
18 "When things don't go as we expected, I ask, 'What can we learn from this experience?'"
23 "I make sure that big projects we undertake are broken down into smaller and doable parts."
28 "I take initiative in experimenting with the way things can be done."

• • •

ACTIVITY: PLANNING WITH THE END IN MIND

Submitted by Blaine Conley

Objectives

Students will be able to:

- Begin to identify issues or challenges in their work or groups that they can find innovative ways to address
- Understand the process of change by working through the problem solving process with the end in mind

Number of Participants

- Any size group.

Time Required

- Minimum 20 minutes

Materials and Equipment

- Internet connection for the YouTube video *Challenge the Process* provided by Bowen Engineering (three Bowen leaders help Bowen to keep moving). Approximately 5 minutes and 30 seconds: http://www.youtube.com/watch?v=s6didZkOhjQ&feature=related
- 3–2–1 Reflection worksheet

Area Setup

- Chairs and tables so that students can work in small groups or pairs

Facilitator Cue: Stress the importance for each student to work through the 3–2–1 Reflection worksheet independently while watching the YouTube video.

Process

1. Pass out the 3–2–1 Reflection worksheet.
2. Play the Bowen Engineering YouTube video: http://www.youtube.com/watch?v=s6didZkOhjQ&feature=related.
3. Students complete the 3–2–1 Reflection worksheet based on what their viewing of the video.

Facilitator Cue: If time allows, you might play the video twice so students can hear the several messages.

4. By using the inspiration from the video, have students identify an area of concern they have in their own course work or a project or group in which they are involved.
5. In small groups or pairs, have students identify their area of concern and share ideas with each other to address each area of concern. Encourage students to use the various behaviors in Challenge the Process to begin to address their areas of concern (e.g., where can they look for unique skills and abilities of members of their groups or others they know that can help?). Where else can they look for new ideas or other innovative ways to do things that will help them address their area (outsight)? How

can they experiment with something new? If the issue is large, how can they break it into smaller pieces to address one at a time?

6. Depending on the time you have, you can have the pairs or small groups share the findings with the entire group. You can begin this process by using the questions in Reflection and Connection to the Model.

Reflection and Connection to the Model

We define *leadership* as the art of mobilizing others to want to struggle for shared aspirations. The struggle comes in not knowing the answer to every challenge. Leaders help people work through problems together, creating space for discussion and discovery. This exercise uses a particular technique for creating that kind of dialogue.

Consider asking students these questions:

- How did the individuals in the video feel when they were Challenging the Process?
- When have you ever felt this way at school?
- What connection do you see between the experience the participants had and The Five Practices of Exemplary Leadership?
- While these individuals talked about their work in a business setting, what relevance does that have to your setting?

Facilitator Cue: The individuals in the video improved their company by taking chances, effectively collaborating, and remaining focused on finding a better way.

Student LPI Behaviors Associated with This Activity

3 "I look for ways to develop and challenge my skills and abilities."
8 "I look for ways that others can try out new ideas and methods."
13 "I search for innovative ways to improve what we are doing."
18 "When things don't go as expected, I ask, 'What can we learn from this experience?'"
23 "I make sure that big projects we undertake are broken down into smaller and doable parts."
28 "I take initiative in experimenting with the way things can be done."

STUDENT WORKSHEET: 3–2–1 REFLECTION

Name:

Three concepts, sentences, or quotes that really stuck out to me:

1.

2.

3.

Two questions that I have:

1.

2.

One thing that I will take back to my group:

1.

ACTIVITY: THE SIX THINKING HATS

Submitted by Stephanie Pearcy

Objectives

Students will be able to:

- Outline at least six methods to use when confronted with obstacles
- Search for new opportunities by considering perspectives other than their own when faced with new challenges and obstacles
- Link the practice of outsight with the six thinking hats process

Number of Participants

- Any size group (ideally groups of 6 each)

Time Required

- 55 minutes

Materials and Equipment

- Newsprint (one piece per person and one for the group activity)
- Red, black, yellow, green, blue, and brown markers—one marker of each of the 6 colors at each table

Area Setup

- Small round tables or grouping with groups of 6 participants

Facilitator Cue: This activity is based on Edward De Bono's original work in *The Six Thinking Hats* and has been adapted here for use with students. It can be used as a one- or two-part activity. The "hats" part of the activity can be replaced by giving participants cards with each color.

Activity adapted from Edward De Bono, *Six Thinking Hats* (Boston: Little Brown, 1985).

Process

1. Give each participant a piece of newsprint and walk them through folding the newsprint into a hat.

Facilitator Cue: Instructions for making the newsprint hat: Hold the paper up vertically; fold in half; turn so the fold is at the top; fold the top left and right corners toward you to make a point; separate the bottom and fold one side toward you; turn it over and fold that side toward you to make a hat.

You can do an Internet search for a process for making a newspaper hat to guide you. This part of the activity can also contribute to learning Challenge the Process by having students think of their own ways to accomplish the task.

2. Have each participant choose a color marker to decorate his or her hat. (If there are fewer than six people in the group, have participants double up on colors.) This is a great icebreaker to begin the activity or meeting and go back to it later.
3. If you have your students make their hats as part of the activity, explain that sometimes we need to step outside our comfort zone and teach ourselves new ways to look at the situation so we can begin developing innovative ways to improve.
4. Once a hat for each color is created at each table, describe the "six thinking hats" and how each one of us must work to think in the different ways at different times. It can be helpful to make a handout for the students describing each hat so they can consult it as they work.
   - Brown = Facts/information
     - What information is available?
     - What facts can you assume based on information given?
     - What absences of information can be identified at this time?
     - This way of thinking is clear-cut: it either is or is not. There is no emotional judgment involved.
   - Red = Feelings/emotions
     - Gut reactions to a situation.
     - Often used to vote for alternatives.
     - Always consider your own feelings and those of unrepresented people who are involved.
   - Black = Being cautious
     - Identifying barriers, hazards, risks, and other negative connotations.
     - Looking for problems and mismatches (critical thinking is "black hat thinking").

  - A natural response for most people—often a barrier to creative solutions and discussions.
  - This is the person who says dismissively, "That won't work," or "We've tried this before."
- Yellow = Positive, optimistic
  - Identifying the benefits of the situation.
  - Identifying the desirable positive outcomes.
  - Looking for reasons to favor something.
  - Opposite of "black hat thinking."
  - Outputs may be statements of the benefits that could be created, likelihood of achievement, identifying key supports available.
- Green = Brand new ideas
  - Brainstorming.
  - Things are said for the sake of seeing what they might mean rather than to form a judgment.
- Blue = The big picture
  - Discussed the thinking process.
  - Each team member will wear it from time to time to figure out how to direct the work together.
  - Should be used at the beginning and end of each thinking session to set objectives, define the route to take, evaluate, and decide where you're going.

Facilitator Cue: It is recommended that each group identify a challenge they are facing (this is easier to do if the activity is conducted with people from the same group). However, group members might not share similar issues in their group or course work, so they might select an issue that faces the entire school or organization. You may choose to have a number of predetermined issues that can be given to the group. Either all groups can work on the same issue (therefore providing the opportunity to see many strategies that were addressed in the exercise and that can be shared at the end), or each group can work on a different issue. The issues or challenges that each group addresses should be relatively similar in complexity. For example, do not have one group address a major issue with academic advising, while another group comes up with a new team mascot name.

Reflection and Connection to the Model

The second commitment of Challenge the Process focuses on how leaders can create an environment where people can learn from experience and from each other. Processes that encourage people to acknowledge different ways of thinking help build that kind of learning environment.

Consider using some or all of these questions to debrief the activity and help students see how to apply different methods and consider new perspectives when faced with challenges or obstacles:

- How did it feel to process from one particular point of view or "hat"? How did you feel being limited to just that hat?
- How did your group function working with each hat being represented? What areas caused struggle?
- How were the "hats" who might have had roles of sharing ideas that created more conflict addressed similarly or differently than those "hats" who seemed to be more congenial or were positive contributors?
- Did the degree of influence differ with various hats? Which ones? What do you think caused this?
- How would this approach help you develop innovative ways to improve your group or organization?
- How is developing new ways of thinking continuous improvement?
- What innovations did your group come up with for addressing your challenge?
- Did you identify any new challenges or obstacles as you discussed your challenge? If so, what were they, and what did you do to address those as well?

Facilitator Cue: It is common when addressing one obstacle that others might crop up. Students need to recognize those and address them rather than ignore them. Watch for groups that focus solely on their original challenge and gloss over anything new they encounter.

- Why is it important to consider different perspectives when developing change or Challenging the Process?
- The term *outsight* refers to our ability to find new ideas in external places, outside our normal purview. How does The Six Hats thinking process allow us to practice outsight?
- When did you find certain hats being supported and certain ones not? How do these types of interactions occur in your groups or others with whom you work, and what, as a leader, do you do about how you react or don't react to certain differences in the various perspectives?

Student LPI Behaviors Associated with This Activity

3 "I look for ways to develop and challenge my skills and abilities."
8 "I look for ways that others can try out new ideas and methods."
13 "I search for innovative ways to improve what we are doing."
18 "When things don't go as expected, I ask, 'What can we learn from this experience?'"
23 "I make sure that big projects we undertake are broken down into smaller and doable parts."
28 "I take initiative in experimenting with the way things can be done."

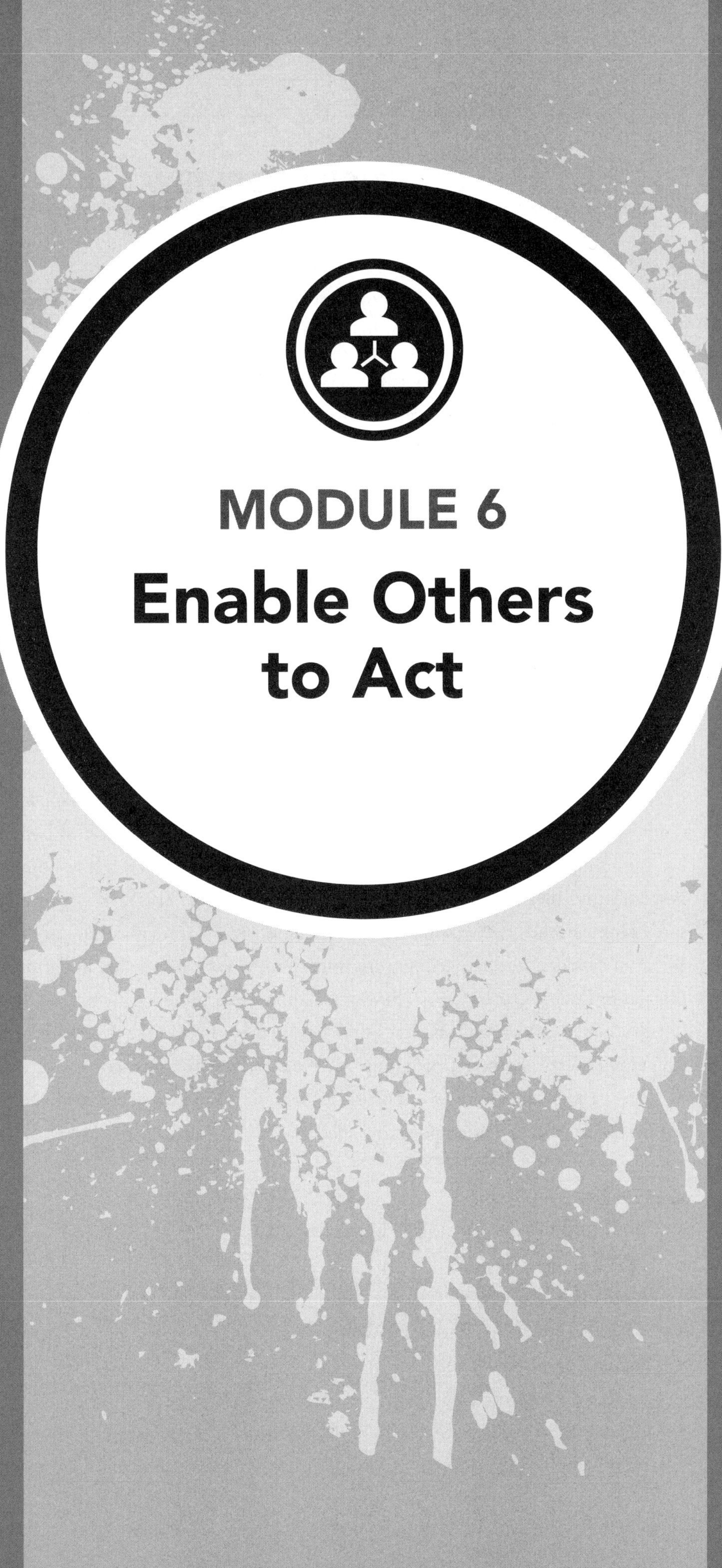

MODULE 6
Enable Others to Act

PRACTICE OVERVIEW

Enable Others to Act: Foster Collaboration and Strengthen Others
Leaders foster collaboration by building trust and facilitating relationships. They strengthen others by enhancing self-determination and developing competence.

Leaders know they can't do it alone. Leadership involves building relationships and requires a group effort. Leaders foster collaboration and create spirited groups. They actively involve others and understand that they have a responsibility to bring others along. Collaboration enables teams, partnerships, and other alliances to function effectively.

Leaders also strengthen the competence and confidence of all members of the team in order for them to feel strong, capable, informed, and connected. They move from being *in control* to *giving over control* to others, becoming their coaches.

WHY STUDENTS SHOULD ENABLE OTHERS TO ACT

Enable Others to Act builds on a basic truth that achieving great things happens not as the result of one person's effort but from the combined efforts of many. This basic truth can be a stumbling block for young leaders who are driven to achieve, feel responsible for the outcome, and therefore decide to act alone. We hear them say, "I'm not sure I can trust some people in the group to do what they're responsible for. It's easier to just do it myself." We've all experienced that feeling from time to time, especially when under pressure. The practice of Enable Others to Act, however, assumes that leaders truly believe that working together achieves more and that they do what it takes to build the trust and confidence to strengthen every member of the group and effectively work together.

These activities provide an opportunity for students to experience firsthand the potential gain of including and empowering others.

Activities List

- The Walk of Peril (or "Indiana Jones's Walk")
- The Captains' Dilemma
- Tennis Ball Madness
- A Picture Is Worth a Thousand Words
- Populating a New Planet
- A Leader's Walk of Trust
- Capture the Dragon
- Help Is on the Way

ACTIVITY: THE WALK OF PERIL (OR "INDIANA JONES'S WALK")

Submitted by Cameron Potter

Objectives

Students will be able to:

- Experience an environment where the only way to succeed is to work collaboratively
- Observe and share what people need to succeed

Number of Participants

- A group size between 8 and 25

Time Required

- 15 to 45 minutes

Materials and Equipment

- Masking tape
- Carpet squares, each 1 foot square (this size can be useful to help with stability)
- A buzzer, whistle, kazoo, or other sound maker

Facilitator Cue: Carpet squares can be replaced with something else as long as the material is not slippery and can sustain the wear and tear of the activity.

Area Setup

- The masking tape should be laid out in a grid of 14-inch squares. The total grid size should not be smaller than 5 by 5 squares and can be up to 10 by 10 squares for larger groups. Place the carpet squares inside each square for stability if desired.

Facilitator Cue: It is important to create a map of the solution to this challenge, as it can be easy to forget or get confused. This map is intended for the facilitator's use only.

Process

1. Start by retelling the scene in the Indiana Jones film *The Search for the Holy Grail*, during which Indiana Jones must step on certain stones in a specific order to get across to the other side. If he steps on the wrong stone, he falls to his death. The students are to recreate this scenario with the grid you have laid out. If you are not familiar with the film, you can describe the grid as a rickety bridge over a raging river: one wrong step, and they fall.
2. Explain that the only way to figure out the pattern is through trial and error. If the group is paying attention to the mistakes the others make, they will learn the pattern quickly and all make it across safely. If they are inattentive to each other or attempting to complete the challenge on their own, they will struggle to complete the activity in the time allowed.
3. Explain that the entire group needs to get from one side to the other, one at a time, without stepping out of sequence in the grid. If they step on the wrong square, they will hear the sound you have designated. They give up their turn and have to start over again from the beginning. They can discuss the pattern only when there is no one trying to cross—no giving step-by-step instructions when someone is on the grid. If someone calls out a hint, use the noisemaker to indicate a "foul" and the person on the grid loses his or her turn.
4. Identify the starting square and the final square.
5. Consider asking the following debriefing questions:
   - What emotions did they feel as a result of "falling off"? This activity is unique in that it not only allows but necessitates "failure" and collaboration. What freedom does this bring to the collaborative process?
   - What role did trust play for the students in this activity?
   - What did they do to help others along? What did others do for them that helped them along?

Variations

- Blindfold various team members and see how the direction-giving changes.
- Create two teams. Then give them the exact directions you would for a single group. Their tendency is to assume it is a competitive situation, so point out that the exercise was never established as a competition. Ask what made them assume it was. What difference did that make in how they approached the problem?
- Introduce the map to one group at some point. There are opportunities for learning to explore during debriefing when a map with the answer is supplied: Who gets the map? Do you give them directions about sharing it or not sharing it? Do you give only one group the map; it so, do they assume they cannot share it?

Reflection and Connection to the Model

Trust is at the core of the first commitment of Enable Others to Act. Leaders understand that trust is key to helping people work in a collaborative way. Leaders also understand that people need to feel both confident and competent to perform at their best. They create an environment where people can gain confidence by learning.

Student LPI Behaviors Associated with This Activity

4 "I foster cooperative rather than competitive relationships among people I work with."
9 "I actively listen to diverse points of view."
14 "I treat others with dignity and respect."
19 "I support the decisions that other people make on their own."
24 "I give others a great deal of freedom and choice in deciding how to do their work."
29 "I provide opportunities for others to take on leadership responsibilities."

Application to Other Practices

When this activity is applied to Challenge the Process, an interesting shift takes place as the activity progresses. While "failure" is expected at the beginning, by the end of the activity everyone should be able to make it across flawlessly. The only way to succeed is to fail and learn from the experience. As a result of the "fail-friendly" atmosphere, the group feels emboldened to act without fear of failure.

• • •

ACTIVITY: THE CAPTAINS' DILEMMA

Submitted by Matthew Eriksen

Objectives:

Students will be able to:

- Articulate the nature and conditions of team experiences that enabled them to act
- Articulate general conditions under which athletic team members are enabled to act
- Develop specific actions they can take to enable their teammates to act

Number of Participants

- Any size group of collegiate athletic team captains
- Can also be used with students leader other kinds of groups

Time Required

- 60 minutes

Facilitator Cue: This activity was designed for sports team captains, but we believe it is equally applicable to students leading other types of groups.

Materials and Equipment

- Whiteboard, chalkboard, or flip chart
- Markers or chalk
- Two sets of handouts with questions for participants: half the group receives the Enabled to Act Group (+) Questions, and the other half of the group receives the Not Enabled to Act (–) Group Questions

Area Setup

- Space arranged space to accommodate students in discussion groups of three

Facilitator Cue: This activity is designed to precede a lecture or discussion of Enable Others to Act. It is intended to help students reflect on experiences in which they were enabled to act. Based on individual and group reflections of these experiences, team captains, or other student leaders, will develop specific actions they can take to create conditions and relationships that will enable teammates to act in a positive, collaborative, trusting way.

Process

1. Create groups with three students per group. Designate half the groups as (+) and explain that they will be exploring team experiences in which they were enabled to act. Designate the other half as (–) and explain they will be exploring team experiences in which they were not enabled to act.

2. Based on the designation of the group—(+) or (–)—distribute the appropriate Group Questions worksheet to each student; there are separate worksheets for the (+) and (–) groups. Explain to the students that they have 10 minutes to answer the worksheet questions on their own.
3. After this self-exploration, ask students to share their answers within their group.
4. Then ask the students to identify common themes among their answers.
5. Thinking about their experiences and the commonalities among them, ask each group to identify three specific actions that they could take as captains of their teams to create conditions under which their teammates would be able to contribute meaningfully to the performance and success of their team.
6. Ask groups to present their three actions and why they believe these actions would be effective in creating conditions that would allow their teammates to contribute meaningfully to the performance and success of their team. Capture these on a flip chart.
7. Ask participants to look at the answers from the enabled group compared to the not-enabled group. What do they notice?

Facilitator Cue: If time permits, you can have each group report out. With less time, you can ask for three of the groups to report. Then ask if there are one or two examples different from the ones captured on the flip chart.

Reflection and Connection to the Model

Leaders understand the importance of taking action and using language that helps people feel confident and supported. What individuals need varies as much as the individuals on a team. Leaders take the time to understand what will make the individual members of the team feel supported. Consider asking students the following questions:

- Why do they think they were asked to engage in this exercise with respect to The Five Practices of Exemplary Leadership model?

Facilitator Cue: Look for an understanding that trust and collaboration are keys for team performance.

- Which of the recommended actions as captains would lead to (1) fostering collaboration by building trust and facilitating relationships or (2) strengthening their teammates by increasing their self-determination and developing their competence, or (3) both?

Facilitator Cue: This is a good transition point into a lecture or discussion on Enable Others to Act. As a follow-up, ask each participant to choose three actions that by the next class or meeting they will take as captains of their teams to create conditions that will allow their teammates to meaningfully contribute to the performance and success of their team.

Student LPI Behaviors Associated with This Activity

4 "I foster cooperative rather than competitive relationships among people I work with."
9 "I actively listen to diverse points of view."
14 "I treat others with dignity and respect."
19 "I support the decisions that other people make on their own."
24 "I give others a great deal of freedom and choice in deciding how to do their work."
29 "I provide opportunities for others to take on leadership responsibilities."

STUDENT WORKSHEET: QUESTIONS FOR THE (+) ENABLED-TO-ACT GROUP

Think about a time when you were on a team and were able to contribute meaningfully to the performance and success of the team with your teammates.

- What conditions were present to make this possible? That is, what was it about the team and nature of the relationships among the players and coach that allowed you and your teammates to meaningfully contribute to the performance and success of the team?

- What conditions or relationships with the coach, captain, and other players made it possible for you specifically to contribute meaningfully to the performance and success of your team? That is, as an individual, why were you able to meaningfully contribute with your teammates to the performance and success of the team?

- What did you think or feel that allowed you to contribute meaningfully to the performance and success of your team?

STUDENT HANDOUT: QUESTIONS FOR THE (–) NOT-ENABLED-TO-ACT GROUP WORKSHEET

Think about a time when you were on a team and were most inhibited from making meaningful contributions to the performance and success of the team with your teammates.

- What conditions existed to create this experience? That is, what was it about the team and nature of the relationship among you and the other players and coach that prohibited you and your teammates from making meaningful contributions to the performance and success of the team?

- What conditions or relationships with the coach, captain, and other players made it impossible for you specifically to contribute meaningfully to the performance and success of your team? That is, as an individual, why were you unable to meaningfully contribute with your teammates to the performance and success of the team?

- What did you think and feel that inhibited you from making meaningful contributions to the performance and success of your team?

ACTIVITY: TENNIS BALL MADNESS

Submitted by Mason Chock

Objectives

Students will be able to:

- Understand the difference between collaborative and competitive relationships
- Experience the impact on a group when leaders help to bring out the best in each person
- Experience the greater benefits and outcomes when a group works together using everyone's individual strengths

Number of Participants

- Minimum 20, maximum 30

Time Required

- 30 to 45 minutes, including debriefing

Materials and Equipment

- 5 hula hoops (or rope or string to create the same diameter "container" as the hula hoop)
- 50 to 150 tennis balls; if tennis balls are unavailable, use foam swimming noodles of about 1 inch in diameter. Cut the noodles into 2-inch sections with a knife, or use soft fuzzy balls about 1 inch in diameter which can be purchased from a craft store.
- Flip chart, whiteboard, or chalkboard, and marker or chart for posting strategies for discussion
- 4 copies of the Rules of Tennis Ball Madness handout in sealed envelopes

Facilitator Cue: You may make up any penalty you wish (e.g., no team action for 30 seconds, forfeit team members, get blindfolded).

Area Setup

- A large open space of about 400 to 500 square feet (e.g., a room measuring 20 feet by 20 feet)

Facilitator Cue: There are some safety concerns to address during the activity:

- Make sure the area you intend to use for this activity is free and clear of holes and anything the students could slip on.
- Remind students of the rules and the top goal of keeping everyone safe: no pushing, tripping, or shoving, for example.

Process

The goal of the activity is to get all the tennis balls from the center container into your container. Each group will have a list of rules. They are as follows:

Rules

- Each person may touch only one ball at a time.
- You may not throw the tennis balls. If you are concerned about participants' agility, you may also add, "You may not roll the tennis balls."
- Once the center container is empty, you may take tennis balls from any other container.
- You may not guard any of the containers.
- You win when all the tennis balls are in your container.
- Violation of a rule results in giving up three tennis balls.

This is how the process works:

1. Divide the group into four equally sized teams (as close as you can get).
2. Supply each team with a hula hoop (or container). Place a fifth hula hoop on the ground (call it the Center). Ask each team to back away to the corners of the space (30 to 40 feet). Each group will then place its hula hoop (or container) on the ground on the borders of the space you have created.
3. Dump 150 tennis balls into the Center hula hoop (or container), and then hand each team a sealed envelope containing the directions (this is the handout). Tell the groups to open the envelope only on your signal so they are all getting the rules at the same time. Remind them the goal of the exercise is to have all the tennis balls in their container.
4. Allow the teams just enough time to read the directions but not process them, and then shout, "Go" (the goal is to force the group to jump into action without planning).
5. Once you have a winner, debrief by forming groups of seven to ten people comprising members from each of the four teams and discussing:
   - Lose-lose, win-lose, win-win (place this on a flip chart visible to all). Ask students which of the strategies they applied produced each of the results listed. Capture those on the appropriate flip chart
   - Share insights as a large group.

Facilitator Cue: Many times, the four groups decide to cooperate by stacking all the hula hoops (or other "containers") and then placing all the balls inside the stack. This is legal according to the rules.

Variation

Keep the number of teams at about seven. If you don't have enough people, do fewer teams, not smaller teams.

Reflection and Connection to the Model

The practice of Enable Others to Act reinforces the notion of collaboration and a leader's commitment to bringing out the best in others based on a deep-seated belief that together we achieve more. The discussion for this activity can point out that lose-lose and win-lose takes much more energy than win-win. Leaders look for win-win from the outset.

Facilitator Cue: You can stoke the fire for this activity by having the small groups do something competitive before you start this exercise. They usually carry that spirit right into Tennis Ball Madness even though the activity is never portrayed as a competition. This can deepen the lesson a bit.

One person can make all the difference in the world. This will usually be an insight when one person is responsible for getting the group to stop the frenzy and come up with a win-win answer (i.e., stack the hula hoops). All it takes is one committed person to see things differently and have the courage, conviction, and support to make their views known to the larger community.

Questions to Discuss

- Can anyone identify an apparent metaphor for the tennis balls and the hula hoops?
- When you heard "Go," you had just enough information to take action. Did that help or hurt your team?

Student LPI Behaviors Associated with This Activity

4 "I foster cooperative rather than competitive relationships among people I work with."
9 "I actively listen to diverse points of view."
14 "I treat others with dignity and respect."

19 "I support the decisions that other people make on their own."
24 "I give others a great deal of freedom and choice in deciding how to do their work."
29 "I provide opportunities for others to take on leadership responsibilities."

Application to Other Practices

This can be applied to Challenge the Process. The assumptions that people make help to point out the way we close ourselves off to new ideas and perspectives. Also, you can point out whether teams had an environment where everyone felt safe to speak, or whether there was a dominant participant who kept people from contributing.

STUDENT HANDOUT: RULES OF TENNIS BALL MADNESS

1. Each person may carry only one item at a time.
2. Items must be carried (no throwing or rolling).
3. Once the center container is empty, you may take items from any other container.
4. You may not guard any of the containers.
5. You win when all the items are in your container.
6. Violation of a rule may result in a penalty.

ACTIVITY: A PICTURE IS WORTH A THOUSAND WORDS

Submitted by Elizabeth Housholder

Objectives

Students will be able to:

- Experience the value of relationship building in the leadership process
- Distinguish the difference between a leader who delegates tasks and one who entrusts his or her followers
- Appreciate the value of and the critical role that Enable Others to Act and trust play in the relational leadership process
- Identify opportunities to Enable Others to Act in one's everyday leadership experiences

Number of Participants

- Ideal for groups of 10 to 20 students

Time Required

- 20 minutes

Materials and Equipment

- Flip chart paper and easel
- Various colored markers
- Optional: Tape, glue, colored construction paper, glitter, scissors

Facilitator Cue: The first piece of flip chart paper is blank. On the second piece, write this quotation: "Grand dreams don't become significant based through the actions of a single person."—James B. Kouzes and Barry Z. Posner.

Area Setup

- Flip chart paper placed on an easel at the center of the room. The first piece of paper is blank; the second piece of flip chart paper has the "Grand dreams don't become significant . . ." quotation written on it in advance.
- The other supplies placed on a table to the side of the room.

Facilitator Cue: This activity has elements of two practices, Enable Others to Act and Inspire a Shared Vision; both are addressed in the debriefing. To begin, after explaining the key tenets of The Five Practices of Exemplary Leadership, explain to the students that they will now explore the role that relationships play in the leadership process and the journey of developing as a leader.

Process

1. State that the group is going to conduct a simulation of leadership in action. Stress the difference between a simulation (an activity that models real-life examples) and a game that holds no distinct purpose.
2. Ask the students to count off by 5s to form groups.
3. Separate the groups so each has its own space.
4. Provide each group one large piece of flip chart paper, markers, and additional supplies as applicable.
5. Tell the students that they will now complete a simulation in which each group draws the same picture using the supplies provided.
6. State the following rules:
   - The facilitator will tell person 1 of each group confidentially what to draw. *Example:* "Draw a scene of 'Freedom' however you envision it."
   - Person 1 is allowed to speak but can give only vague directions without stating what exactly to draw. For example, person 1 would say to team members: "Draw a large circle and lines coming out of the circle," not, "Draw the sun."
   - Persons 2 to 5 together create the scene person 1 has instructed them to make, but they are not allowed to communicate through spoken words.
7. Ask each group to identify a leader (this is person 1) and tell each leader privately what the scene is that the group members will draw.
8. Allow 5 minutes for completing the activity, observing the dynamics of each group and the picture's formation process. Give the groups a 1-minute warning.
9. Once the time is complete, ask the groups to have their leaders share the group's picture.

Facilitator Cue: Note the differences in the pictures and the level of creativity, complexity, and completion without judgment.

10. After debriefing, flip the page over to the sheet that was prewritten with the "Grand dreams" quote. Have participants reflect silently.
11. Go around the room and have each participant state one adjective to describe how he or she feels after this activity—for example: *empowered, energized, challenged.*

Reflection and Connection to the Model

Creating a compelling image of the future is how leaders engage others in hopes for times ahead. In order for it to be compelling, it must resonate with others. Leaders understand that in order to be successful, they must know the values of the people they hope to engage; they must learn what moves them, inspires them, and speaks to them. Having this knowledge is the foundation not only for the practice of Inspire a Shared Vision but also for Enable Others to Act. It leads to relationships characterized by trust, collaboration, and interdependence.

Questions to Discuss

- The saying goes, "A picture is worth a thousand words." What words describe what you think happened when each group created its picture?
- Was your group successful? Why or why not?
- What was it like being the leader of the group with the vision but limited in ways to communicate that vision? What was your strategy in engaging your group members to help? Did you communicate and ask for their feedback in how to create the picture?
- What was it like to be the followers? How did you feel when you couldn't receive clear instructions on what to draw? Did you feel like a valued member? Why or why not?
- In an ideal setting, how would the leader and the followers go about doing this task? Why do you think this would be a better strategy?
- Enable Others to Act requires collaboration, trust, listening, interdependence, and empowerment. Think about your own leadership experiences. What are the challenges of Enable Others to Act in real-life scenarios?
- Think about the terms *delegating* and *entrusting*. Do you see a distinction between them? Which is more powerful and positive in building relationships with our team members? Why?
- What are the key lessons from this experience? What commitments can you make today to help you Enable Others to Act?

Student LPI Behaviors Associated with This Activity

4 "I foster cooperative rather than competitive relationships among people I work with."
9 "I actively listen to diverse points of view."
14 "I treat others with dignity and respect."
19 "I support the decisions that other people make on their own."
24 "I give others a great deal of freedom and choice in deciding how to do their work."
29 "I provide opportunities for others to take on leadership responsibilities."

ACTIVITY: POPULATING A NEW PLANET

Submitted by Scott Dover and Angie Vyverberg Chapln

Objectives

Students will be able to:

- Apply communication and negotiation techniques
- Work as a team to achieve a unified outcome

Number of Participants

- Any size group that can be subdivided into smaller groups of 3 to 4 individuals

Time Required

- 45 to 60 minutes

Materials and Equipment

- Copies of the New Planet Activity Sheet handout for each participant
- Easel, flip chart, and markers

Area Setup

- Seats at a table
- An easel, flip chart, and markers for each table

Facilitator Cue: Initiate the activity with an explanation of Enable Others to Act, emphasizing the role of trust and collaboration in the face of challenges and in pursuit of a future vision based on shared values.

Process

1. Divide the group into random teams of three or four people.
2. Tell the teams this story:

> Due to the pollution in the air, the Earth's ozone layer is way too thin. Days are getting hotter and hotter. In a couple of days, the Earth is going to be too hot for humans to survive. NASA has a rocket that will send people to a new planet so that they can repopulate and the human species will not become extinct. The only problem is that the rocket can take only 10 people!!!

3. Distribute the New Planet Activity Sheet handout—one for each student
4. Allow teams 25 to 30 minutes to discuss and decide which ten individuals on the activity sheet they will select to make the trip to the new planet. The team should record their choices on the flip chart.
5. Ask each team to delegate a representative to share their list and provide a brief explanation as to why they selected whom they did.
6. The facilitator will tally how many times a particular individual is selected.

Reflection and Connection to the Model

Leaders help others work effectively together. They allow others to explore possibilities and make room for many perspectives and opinions. This activity helps students experience group decision-making and learning in the process what it takes to create one voice from many.

Questions to Discuss

- How did your team make decisions? Do you feel as though everyone was heard?
- What communication techniques did you use to facilitate your selections?
- What were some of the challenges?
- How did the team handle conflict?
- Did a leader emerge?
- What other leadership behaviors and practices did you observe?
- In this activity, you were creating a group with the hope that they would be able to work collaboratively. Can you point out some examples of that?
- What other behaviors did you observe that were consistent with Enable Others to Act?

Student LPI Behaviors Associated with This Activity

4 "I foster cooperative rather than competitive relationships among people I work with."
9 "I actively listen to diverse points of view."
14 "I treat others with dignity and respect."
19 "I support the decisions that other people make on their own."
24 "I give others a great deal of freedom and choice in deciding how to do their work."
29 "I provide opportunities for others to take on leadership responsibilities."

Application to Other Practices

This can also apply to Challenge the Process. There are many opportunities to explore the assumptions we make about what the new planet will be like. Ask the group to go through the same process but debrief by asking them to acknowledge their own assumptions (for example: Did they select a botanist hoping she could help them grow things assuming the planet had vegetation?)

STUDENT HANDOUT: NEW PLANET ACTIVITY SHEET

Due to the pollution in the air, the Earth's ozone layer is way too thin. Days are getting hotter and hotter. In a couple of days, the Earth is going to be too hot for humans to survive. NASA has a rocket that will send people to a new planet so that they can repopulate and the human species will not become extinct...the only problem is the rocket can only take ten people!

Talk to your group and decide which ten people should go to the new planet:

1. 35-year-old female, has three children, graphic artist
2. 12-year-old male, straight A student, wants to be a police officer
3. 59-year-old male, computer technician
4. 18-year-old male, high school drop-out, does not have a job
5. 24-year-old female, pregnant and expecting twins
6. 25-year-old female, fashion model
7. 15-year-old female, pregnant, high school student
8. 16-year-old male, boyfriend of #7, baby's father
9. 30-year-old male, garbage collector, has wife
10. 21-year-old male, photographer, single
11. 70-year-old male, retired lawyer
12. 50-year-old female, doctor, cannot have children
13. 45-year-old male, investment banker, very wealthy
14. 40-year-old male, dentist
15. 22-year-old female, college student, studying the environment
16. 30-year-old male, famous actor, known to use drugs
17. 14-year-old female, soccer player, has part-time job as cashier
18. 38-year-old male, pilot and astronaut, has the flu
19. 29-year-old female, botanist (studies plants/trees)
20. 49-year-old male, governor of California
21. 27-year-old male, reporter for the local newspaper
22. 30-year-old female, cook, owns her own restaurant
23. 10-year-old male, farmer
24. 60-year-old female, astronomer
25. 52-year-old male, fisherman
26. 49-year-old female, aircraft repairwoman
27. 22-year-old female, singer, dancer, actress, smoker
28. 28-year-old male, professional basketball player
29. 33-year-old male, carpenter, has the chicken pox
30. 28-year-old female, psychologist, counselor, has fear of flying

ACTIVITY: A LEADER'S WALK OF TRUST

Submitted by Craig Haptonstall

Objectives

Students will be able to:

- Understand that establishing trust happens through actions more than words
- Explore the meaning of the word *trust* for themselves and others

Number of Participants

- Any size group

Time Required

- 10 to 20 minutes depending on the size of the group

Materials and Equipment

- None

Area Setup

- Enough space for people to get up and move around to meet the other participants

Facilitator Cue: This exercise is best done after students have had a chance to work together or get to know each other. If you have the same group of students for a long period of time, this is a good midway check-in to see how the group is doing in the "trust" department.

Process

1. Ask students to stand up and prepare to talk to the other participants.
2. Tell them this is a challenge by choice: they are allowed to select whom they will encounter, but the goal is to have everyone encounter everyone else.

3. As they meet each person, they are to say one of three things and nothing else:
   - "I trust you."
   - "I don't trust you."
   - "I don't care to say."
4. People will be immediately struck by the dilemma of what to say and how truthful to be in their communications. After all the encounters and communications take place, debrief with questions like this one:
   - "How did that go?" If they say it was uncomfortable, which is likely, explore why. Then ask, "What would have made it more comfortable?"

Facilitator Cue: One thing that will surface is that being able to say only those three things seemed unfair to everyone and might even build distrust. Without accompanying reasoning, we are left with more unanswered questions.

- Did anyone say anything other than "I trust you"?
- If you said, "I trust you," to people, what did you mean? You trust them with what?

Reflection and Connection to the Model

A leadership challenge for all leaders is to communicate trust in their everyday actions. The words are shallow without supporting evidence. What is most interesting about this activity is that it allows people to experience the dilemma of how truthful to be and what it means to communicate trust. These three messages—"I trust you," "I don't trust you," and "I don't care to say"—capture the meanings people are getting from your everyday actions. What matters more than your words are the actions you take. Those are the messages you send out loud and clear.

Since trust is developmental dynamic that works from the inside out, leaders must elevate their own ability to be vulnerable and trust others before they can raise their level of trust. This is at the heart of the first commitment of Enable Others to Act: foster collaboration by building trust and facilitating relationships.

Student LPI Behaviors Associated with This Activity

4 "I foster cooperative rather than competitive relationships among people I work with."
14 "I treat others with dignity and respect."
24 "I give others a great deal of freedom and choice in deciding how to do their work."

ACTIVITY: CAPTURE THE DRAGON

Submitted by Kelly Jordan

Objectives

Students will be able to:

- Emphasize the value of trust among collaborators
- Demonstrate the worth of collaboration among groups
- Illustrate the ability of cooperation and collaborative actions to strengthen others and the synergy of cooperation

Number of Participants

- Up to 32 participants

Time Required

- 20 to 40 minutes

Materials and Equipment

- Some method of random selection of four units (e.g., dice, cards, slips of paper) to determine the order of the draw (referred to below in greater detail).
- A bag and seven slips of paper—one slip for each team, numbered in order for choosing their turn. (This is to produce the appropriate odds of either 1:3, 1:4, 1:5, or 1:6, with the 1:6 option requiring seven slips of paper; referred to in detail below.)
- Prop of some creature to serve as the "dragon."
- Enough baked goods for each participant to have one.

Area Setup

- Participants stand in a diamond shape, with one team on each side and the prop in the middle

Process

The background of this activity is that the dragon represents the sum of all that is good and desirable for the group participating in the activity (whatever that may be), and the only way to obtain these benefits (represented by the task's reward) is to capture the dragon.

A plate of cookies (or some other desirable treat with enough for each participant) represents the benefits of capturing the dragon.

The goal of the exercise is to capture the dragon:

- If one team captures the dragon on its own, it receives all the benefits (e.g., cookies), with multiple cookies for each person.
- If the teams collaborate and capture the dragon together, they share all the benefits (i.e., the cookies), meaning that each member receives a lesser share (one cookie each) than if the team captured the dragon on its own.
- If a member tries to capture the dragon and fails, the dragon will escape and no one will receive any benefits.
- If all teams agree to take successive steps forward and not try to capture the dragon on their own, they will lose enough by turn 6 to guarantee successful collective capture of the dragon (and receive one cookie each).

How the Game Works

Each team (sitting or standing)is positioned around the dragon, forming a diamond and preventing the dragon from escaping. On the game's first turn, no team has access to a metaphorical "magic lasso," meaning that the only choice each team can make is to take an actual or metaphorical step forward (if the participants are standing, they can take a step forward; if they are sitting, they can take a metaphorical step forward by moving their chairs or desks forward).

On the game's second turn, the team that goes first metaphorically receives a magic lasso they can use to capture the dragon. The odds of using the magic lasso successfully are highest during the team's first turn in possession of the lasso (one in three) and steadily decrease with each successive turn (one in four, then one in five, and finally one in six for the team that possesses the magic lasso for four turns and thus incentivizing the use of the magic lasso as soon as one's team is able to do so).

Facilitator Cue: Facilitators can make use of any object they deem appropriate to represent the magic lasso, but there is no requirement to do so. If a prop is not used, the facilitator simply announces when each team comes into possession of its own metaphorical "magic lasso" with enough impact to ensure all participants are made aware and understand the implications.

The goal is to "capture" the dragon in one of two ways:

1. Collaborating as teams to take enough actual or metaphorical steps forward so that the teams collapse the diamond around the dragon so closely that the dragon is "captured"

by the proximity of the teams (i.e., the dragon has nowhere to go and so must surrender to the combined presence of the teams). Each team receives a portion of the task's overall reward.

2. Acting independently by taking a chance of using the magic lasso to metaphorically capture the dragon for one's own team. The team that captures the dragon receives the entire task's reward for themselves.

The first approach, a collaborative one, is guaranteed to succeed by turn 6 of the game and will result in each team's receiving a portion of the task's overall reward. The second approach, an independent one, may or may not work, depending on the outcome of the attempt. If the outcome is unsuccessful, the game ends with the dragon escaping and no team receives any of the task's reward. To provide a bit more incentive to succeed in the task, you can tell the participants that the reward will be shared with others not participating and with whom they would not want to receive the reward!

The game consists of each team making a deliberate decision during each turn. The decision can be only one of two things: (1) take a step forward or (2) try to capture the dragon. They capture the dragon by being able to touch it. If they have the magic lasso, they do not need to be close; if they don't get the magic lasso, it benefits them to get physically closer.

The teams use the method of random selection (e.g., rolling the dice with the highest number going first, drawing cards with the highest value going first, drawing slips of paper with number written on them with the highest number going first) to determine the order of progression among the teams. Once the team going first is determined, the order proceeds around the diamond in a clockwise direction.

At the beginning of the exercise and during turn 1, no team has possession of the magic lasso. Beginning with turn 2, the first team in the order of draw has the option of trying to capture the dragon on its own or take an actual or metaphorical step forward.

As already noted, the odds of success for each team's individual attempts to capture the dragon are highest on the first turn they obtain possession of the magic lasso and decrease with each successive turn. The activity is designed to incentivize teams to consider acting independently most seriously on the first turn they obtain possession of the magic lasso so that teams cross a decisive threshold at the end of turn 5 and that their collective efforts to capture the dragon on turn 6 are guaranteed to be successful if they can perpetuate the collective collaboration to this turn in the game.

If a team elects to try to capture the dragon on its own, the facilitator, in full view of all teams, puts one slip of paper marked "Success" in a bag or other container and the requisite number of other slips of paper marked "Fail" (either two to produce the one-in-three odds, three to produce the one-in-four odds, four to produce the one-in-five odds, or five to produce the one-in-six odds) into the bag or container with the "Success" slip of paper (make a big show of this process to ensure all participants understand what is occurring and the odds that are at stake).

One member of the team then is allowed to draw one slip of paper from the bag or other container and shares the results with the entire group. If the participant draws the slip of paper marked "Success," the facilitator gives that group the task's reward for them to share only with their teammates (make a big show of this process as well). If the participant draws a slip of paper marked "Fail," the facilitator takes the dragon and has it physically "fly" over the team that tried to capture it and out of the diamond. The facilitator then takes the task's reward and moves it physically out of the room, telling the participants to whom it will be delivered (again, make a big show of the process for effect).

If any team attempts to capture the dragon on its own, the activity ends, regardless of the outcome, and the debriefing begins based on the outcome.

When conducting the exercise, provide the team that has the option of making a choice some time to deliberate and discuss their decision.

You may have to help the group move toward a decision by applying a false sense of urgency (e.g., "The dragon is getting nervous, so you need to make a decision within the next minute").

Here is the process to follow:

1. Divide the group into four teams (the teams need not be equal in numbers, but should be close).
2. Have the teams determine the order of progression using dice, cards, or slips of paper. Once the team going first is determined, the order of progression proceeds clockwise around the diamond.
3. Explain the context and rules of the activity, and ensure the teams understand them.
4. Conduct turn 1. No team has the opportunity to try to capture the dragon, so the only choice they have is to take one step forward.
5. Conduct turn 2. Team 1 has the opportunity to try to capture the dragon for themselves with a one-in-three chance of success or take one actual or metaphorical step forward. Teams 2, 3, and 4 can elect only to step forward. If team 1 elects to try to capture the dragon and is successful, the team receives all of the cookies; if team 1 elects to try to capture the dragon and fails, the dragon escapes and no one on any team gets any cookies.
6. Conduct turn 3. Team 1 has the opportunity to capture the dragon for themselves with a one-in-four chance of success, or take one actual or metaphorical step forward, and team 2 has the opportunity to capture the dragon for themselves with a one-in-three chance of success, or take one actual or metaphorical step forward. Team 1 makes its selection, followed by team 2, and then teams 3 and 4 have only the choice of taking one actual or metaphorical step forward. If team 1 or team 2 elects to try to capture the dragon and is successful, the team receives all of the cookies for themselves. If teams 1 or 2 elect to try to capture the dragon and fail, the dragon escapes and no one on any team gets any cookies.

7. Conduct turn 4. Teams 1, 2, and 3 have the opportunity to capture the dragon for themselves. Team 1's odds for success decrease to one in five, team 2's odds of success decrease to one in four, and team 3 has the opportunity to capture the dragon for themselves with a one-in-three chance of success. Team 1 decides either to try to capture the dragon or take a step forward; team 2 decides either to try to capture the dragon or take a step forward; and team 3 decides either to try to capture the dragon or take a step forward. Team 1 makes its selection, followed by teams 2 and 3, and then team 4 has only the choice of taking one step forward. If team 1, 2, or 3 elects to try to capture the dragon and is successful, the team receives all of the cookies. If teams 1, 2, or 3 elect to try to capture the dragon and fail, the dragon escapes and no one on any team gets any cookies.
8. Conduct turn 5. All four teams now have the opportunity to capture the dragon for themselves and thus have legitimate choices to make between trying to capture the dragon for themselves and taking a step forward. Team 1's odds for success decrease to one in six, team 2's odds of success decrease to one in five, team 3's odds for success decrease to one in four, and team 4 has the opportunity to capture the dragon for themselves with a one-in-three chance of success. Team 1 decides either to try to capture the dragon or take a step forward; team 2 decides either to try to capture the dragon or take a step forward; then team 3 decides either to try to capture the dragon or take a step forward, and finally team 4 decides either to try to capture the dragon or take a step forward .

Facilitator Cue: By step 8 in the exercise, the members of team 4 are quite anxious, and the facilitator should make use of this emotion to heighten the sense of choice for all. The members of team 4 are perhaps most amenable to trying to capture the dragon for themselves during this turn, when their team's odds of success for acquiring the entire task's reward for themselves are at their highest and realizing that turn 6 will result in their having to share the task's reward with the other teams.

Team 1 makes its selection, followed by teams 2, 3, and 4. If any team elects to try to capture the dragon and is successful, the team receives all of the cookies. If any team elects to try to capture the dragon and fails, the dragon escapes and no one on any team gets any cookies. This is a critical turn in the game: waiting to the next turn guarantees that the dragon will be captured, although it means that each team will receive only a portion of the task reward.

9. Conduct turn 9. All four teams have the opportunity to capture the dragon for themselves with a 100 percent chance of success (i.e., the odds for each a team are one in one, meaning that only the slip of paper marked "Success" is placed in the bag or other container, ensuring a successful draw any each and every team), having crossed the decisive threshold All participants get a cookie.

Facilitator Cue: The decisive threshold in step 9 is another event device designed to hold out the guaranteed chance for success if all teams can collaborate to reach turn 6 by changing the conditions of the game and bring it to an end.

Reflection and Connection to the Model

Enable Others to Act is the practice that leaders rely on when they face challenges. It allows them to help people bring out their best in support of the group's vision. It is about working collaboratively and building trusting relationships. This activity helps to explore those relationships and how they develop.

Questions for Discussion

- How did your team make decisions? Do you feel as though everyone heard?
- What communication techniques were used to facilitate your selections?
- How did the team handle conflict?
- Was it a truly collaborative effort?
- What other leadership behaviors and practices did you observe?
- What other behaviors did you observe that were consistent with Enable Others to Act?

Student LPI Behaviors Associated with This Activity

4 "I foster cooperative rather than competitive relationships among people I work with."
9 "I actively listen to diverse points of view."
14 "I treat others with dignity and respect."
19 "I support the decisions that other people make on their own."
29 "I provide opportunities for others to take on leadership responsibilities."

• • •

ACTIVITY: HELP IS ON THE WAY

Submitted by Beth High

Objectives

Students will be able to:

- Explore the challenges of working collaboratively
- Explore the benefits of working collaboratively

- Identify the behaviors that encourage collaborative work
- Recognize the impact of their words
- Identify the leadership qualities they bring to a team
- Identify the leadership qualities others bring to a team

Number of Participants

- 8 to 48 participants

Time Required

- 60 to 90 minutes

Facilitator Cue: Depending on the model you chose, it can be fun and helpful to have a story associated with the activity to establish a sense of urgency and to support the goal of working together. Here is one example for a helicopter:

> Your team is on a special mission to deliver medicine and food supplies in a helicopter [or all-terrain vehicle or something else depending on the model you select] to a remote area that been struck by a natural disaster. On the way, the helicopter hits a raging storm and goes down. The members of the crew who survive include the pilot of the helicopter who was along to help train the local pilot. He has a schematic of the helicopter and a clear picture of it from several angles. He believes there are enough parts scattered about the crash site to reassemble the helicopter and use some fuel from the original vehicle to get to safety. You have only 30 minutes to find the pieces and assemble the vehicle because the fuel is slowly leaking from the original tank and will be lost.

The benefit of using a story is that it adds the urgency and a sense of fun to the activity. However, you don't want students sidetracked by it with comments like, "Why don't we just use our cell phones and call for help?" It can be helpful to point this out and ask your students to buy into the fun. If that doesn't seem possible, the activity can be done without a story.

Materials and Equipment

- 2 to 7 matching models of some kind of unit of transportation (helicopter, bus, race car) made out of plastic interlocking bricks
- Poster board or cardboard

Area Setup

- Enough space for teams of 8 people to assemble the transportation model they choose.
- Space to display the assembled model. The space needs to be close enough to the other tables for a representative from each group to be able to walk to the table to observe the model closely. The model needs to be hidden from the view of the rest of the group. Using poster board or cardboard braced to stand on its edge is a simple solution to shield the model from view from all but the assigned observer.

Process

Before the Activity

1. You will need one completely assembled model.
2. You will need additional unassembled models—one for each group of eight students.
3. Depending on the number of groups, you may need to find additional people to support the activity as observers who will make sure the rules are followed and observe the groups' behavior for the debriefing.
4. Divide the pieces at each table so that each participant has an assortment of pieces.

Facilitator Cue: There are variations you can use such as putting the pieces into bags and hiding them around the space (remember you said the team had to scavenge for the pieces), or you can put them in the center of the table in one large pile and see how the team divides them.

When Students Arrive

5. Assign students to their groups, and begin your instruction. Give one copy of the activity rules on the student handout to each group. It is best to keep the model parts away from the students in some way until all the relevant information is read.
6. Begin the timing (allow extra time if you have them also searching for the parts)
7. For the debriefing, gather all crews together to reflect on the experience with questions such as these:
   - What went well?
   - What didn't?

- Who on you team said something memorable or helpful? What did that person say (as specifically as you can remember) and why did it help?
- If you did this again, what would you do differently?

Facilitator Cue: The observers can be part of this debriefing. They can help fill in the details that others don't remember. It is a good idea to let the crew speak first, but then it can be useful to ask the observers the first three questions in step 7 of the process.

Reflection and Connection to the Model

When faced with challenges that arise as a result of pursuing a common goal, leaders understand that working collaboratively and building relationships grounded in trust is key to success. All members of the team need to bring all of their skills and knowledge to the table, and leaders make space for that to happen. This activity helps to explore the roles students play on teams and how they develop through the actions they choose to take.

Questions for Discussion

- How did your team make decisions? Do you feel as though everyone was heard?
- Did a single leader emerge, or were there multiple leaders?

Facilitator Cue: The definition of collaboration is that it produces results that would not be possible without the participation of every member. Cooperation means that members work well together. Which was demonstrated during this activity?

- What other leadership behaviors and practices did you observe?
- What behaviors that we've discussed are consistent with Enable Others to Act?
- Did you take advantage of the strengths in the group?
- Did you discover any new strengths in the group? Describe those and how you saw them demonstrated.
- How did the team handle conflict?
- Was it a truly collaborative effort? If so, can you identify the one thing each crew member contributed that allowed success to be possible?

Student LPI Behaviors Associated with This Activity

4 "I foster cooperative rather than competitive relationships among people I work with."
9 "I actively listen to diverse points of view."
14 "I treat others with dignity and respect."
19 "I support the decisions that other people make on their own."
24 "I give others a great deal of freedom and choice in deciding how to do their work."
29 "I provide opportunities for others to take on leadership responsibilities."

Application to Other Practices

This can be applied to Inspire a Shared Vision. In order for a vision to be shared, each person pursuing that vision must have a clear sense of what is being pursued, a clear image that he or she can align with, and how he or she can contribute to it in a unique way. This exercise can help students see how important it is to be clear on expressing what they see and listen attentively to the questions and ideas others have to ensure they are all seeing the same thing.

STUDENT HANDOUT: "HELP IS ON THE WAY" RULES

- Until you are ready to start assembly, you may not exchange the pieces, put any pieces together, or line them up in any orderly manner.
- Each crew member may handle only the parts that are placed in front of him or her. Once the parts have been assembled into subassemblies (two or more parts), the other crew members may handle the parts. You will notice some pieces are already glued or assembled. Do not take them apart and consider them as one part.
- You cannot fake subassemblies and give them to one team member to assemble.
- Only one crew member at a time may view the schematic (the assembled model that is hidden from view) on the observation table. While the crew member is at the observation table, he or she must have no communication, verbal or visual, with the rest of the crew.
- No one may touch the model. Your crew may have a total of fourteen views of the model. The component you are trying to assemble may not be taken to the observation table.
- Your crew has one or more designated observers. It is the observer's job to make sure the groups are following the rules. He or she will not answer any questions.
- When you feel your helicopter [or other vehicle] is ready for action—in other words, it is an exact replica of the assembled model—you can request that your observer inspect it. The observer will inform the crew if they have been successful, but nothing else. He or she will not supply any hints.
- Use only verbal communication (no writing or note taking allowed).
- Assembly must take place at the crew's table. You cannot collaborate with other crews unless given permission.

MODULE 7

Encourage the Heart

PRACTICE OVERVIEW

Encourage the Heart: Recognize Contributions and Celebrate the Values and Victories
Leaders recognize contributions by showing appreciation for individual excellence. They celebrate the values and victories by creating a spirit of community.

Making extraordinary things happen in groups and organizations is hard work. The climb to the top is arduous and long, and as people become exhausted, frustrated, or disenchanted along the way, they're often tempted to give up. Genuine acts of caring uplift the spirit and draw people forward. To keep hope and determination alive, leaders recognize the contributions that individuals make. On every winning team, the members need to share in the rewards of their collective efforts, so leaders celebrate group accomplishments. They make people feel like heroes.

WHY STUDENTS SHOULD ENCOURAGE THE HEART

Exemplary leaders understand that all people need to feel valued, feel they are part of something, and have a clear sense of purpose. Student leaders strive to provide that for the group and start by always being on the lookout for what people do that supports the values and the vision of the group and helps move everyone closer to their shared goal. They make it their job to catch others in the act of doing things right and then recognize them in a meaningful and genuine way, providing the sense of value and purpose that the individual needs. These activities give students the practice they need keeping their eyes and ears wide open for what happens around them that is worthy of recognition.

Leaders also strive to recognize people publicly and celebrate group accomplishments. This reinforces the vision and values for the group and creates a sense of community. The activities in this module help students experience the benefits of creating community and give them a chance to connect to others in a new way with intention and a sense of purpose.

Activities List

- Compliment Swap
- Praise
- Identifying Individual Recognition Tactics
- Encourage the Heart Party Time with Your Group
- Recognition Car Wash
- Recognition Speed Dating
- Good Vibrations
- Web of Yarn

ACTIVITY: COMPLIMENT SWAP

Submitted by Leah Flynn

Objectives

Students will be able to:

- Understand the importance of providing valuable feedback and encouragement to their fellow team members
- Identify tools to provide effective and (fun!) feedback to team members, colleagues, and others
- Learn about encouraging, motivating, and celebrating accomplishments

Number of Participants

- Any size group

Time Required

- 20 minutes

Materials and Equipment

- Index cards (several per student)
- Paper bags with each participant's name written on the front of each bag
- Small pieces of scrap paper for "warm-fuzzy" notes
- Writing tools

Area Setup

- Setup that is conducive for the participants to work in pairs as well as be able to move around the room easily
- Space to move chairs to the side if need be.

Facilitator Cue: Use this activity as a warm-up to a presentation on Encourage the Heart. The last steps of the process should be enacted at the end of the workshop (or day, week, or weekend) when participants have gotten to know each other.

Process

1. Each student receives an index card.
2. The facilitator instructs students to write down two items on their index card, with a 5- to 7-minute deadline:
   - A memorable or best compliment or act of recognition (or both) that they have received from, a team member. organization member, leader of a group, or advisor.
   - A memorable or best compliment or act of recognition (or both) they have provided to a team member, a fellow employee, a supervisee, or a colleague in the past. Examples of recognition are an award; recognition at a group dinner, event, or meeting; an e-mail from an officer or other member of the organization; or a simple compliment shared in passing at a meeting, an event or a team program.
3. Have each person choose a partner.
4. Partners swap compliments with each other over 5 minutes so that they can share meaningful practices for providing feedback or recognition (this is illustrated by the recognition the person gave to someone else and as well as by the recognition they received from someone else).
   - For those who shared recognition they received, ask, "How did the compliment or recognition make you feel?"
   - For those who shared a time when they gave recognition, ask, "How did it make the person feel that you gave a compliment or recognition to this person?"
   - How do these acts inspire your work as a leader or member?
5. Each member of the group is instructed to find another partner and repeat step 4. Depending on the amount of time available, students will repeat step 4 two or more times with new partners, so that they have heard and shared a good number of compliments with the people in the room.
6. Collect the index cards to create a summary of the recognition practices others have used; you will redistribute them to the group later.

Facilitator Cue: If the group does not meet again, add some time at the end of the activity to have students share the best examples they heard.

Variation

Facilitator Cue: The variation on this activity can occur after the workshop or session where you used this activity if the group continues to meet.

At the end of the workshop (or throughout the program if you choose), hang the paper bags with the students' names on them somewhere that is visible to them (perhaps in the group's office, a main meeting room, or lounge). Students are encouraged to write "compliments" to their peers throughout the activity and place in the recipient's bag. *Examples:* "I love your enthusiasm!" "Your team members are lucky to have someone who is so thoughtful!" "Good luck on that project you are working on. I know you will do great!"

Take down all of these "warm fuzzy" bags at the end of the workshop or retreat (after a determined period of time) and return each to the appropriate student to take home.

Facilitator Cue: For future conversations with the group about Encourage the Heart:

- Genuine feedback and motivation are important to encouraging others in their work. It is important to listen and understand the work that each member in your group does in order to provide genuine feedback.
- Encourage the Heart involves celebrating the values and victories of the group and recognizing the contributions a person has made to the effort.
- Having a "recipe" list for providing compliments can be a good tool for some to have as some people may get stuck on what it means to provide a compliment or what makes for a genuinely thoughtful one. For example, ask your students to think about a specific act they can acknowledge or recognize someone else for, what they appreciated about that contribution, and how they thought that particular contribution made a difference to them, others, or the group or project as a whole. Students often forget the feelings that they experience when someone recognizes them for their hard work and accomplishments. It is important for leaders to keep those good feelings in mind in order to continue to motivate and encourage other team members' good work.

Reflection and Connection to the Model

Leaders understand that acknowledgment needs to be both meaningful and genuine. Shallow praise or insincere compliments don't draw people together and in fact can have an effect that is the opposite of what is intended. This activity helps students see how genuine and meaningful recognition makes a difference in how others become more committed to and engaged in the group.

Questions for Discussion

- What were some of your favorite compliments or recognitions that you heard from your conversations?
- How might the compliments or recognitions you heard and shared help in your work with your group and team?
- At what point in your project, program, or work do you think that Encouraging the Heart would be useful?

Student LPI Behaviors Associated with This Activity

5 "I praise people for a job well done."
10 "I encourage others as they work on activities and programs in our organization."
15 "I express appreciation for the contributions that people make."
30 "I make sure that people are creatively recognized for their contributions."

• • •

ACTIVITY: PRAISE

Submitted by Lori McClurg

Objectives

Students will be able to:

- Become comfortable with giving praise and showing appreciation for individual excellence
- Experience the impact associated with giving praise to others and how it affects the individual as well as the group (if applicable)

Number of Participants

- Any size group

Time Required

- 5 to 15 minutes, depending on the size of the group

Materials and Equipment

- Access to e-mail and connection to various social media outlets

Area Setup

- No special setup; this activity is done outside the classroom or regular group meeting

Facilitator Cue: Set the stage as to why students will be doing this assignment by having them envision a situation such as working for a boss or someone else who never gave or gives praise but easily and quickly points out when an error is made. You might initially explore with your students the various reasons that people don't give praise or encouragement to others. Maybe the boss or leader does this because he or she believes the other person knows he or she is doing a good job so doesn't need to be told. Ask students how that feels.

Now have students envision being in a position of leadership (perhaps even several years into their career) when they are starting to lead or manage other people. Talk about what causes some to forget to acknowledge others. What are the contributing factors in ignoring this important practice? For example, if this person doesn't usually acknowledge others, it might initially be uncomfortable to start doing this all of a sudden. This activity is intended to help students get comfortable with praising.

Keep in mind that while this activity has students recognizing others in ways other than face-to-face, its primary purpose is to help students begin to understand the importance of giving recognition and get into the habit of doing so often and in ways in which they might initially be more comfortable doing so.

Process

1. Students are to give praise to three people. This can be done in person (where it has a greater impact) but can also be done using social media or directly through e-mail.
2. Once they give the praise, they send the instructor or advisor an e-mail with the explanation of the praise.
3. Advise students to accept the praise in the manner given.

4. Instruct students to keep the behaviors and spirit of Encourage the Heart in mind when offering praise: the praise should be genuine and meaningful and not simply a compliment such as, "I like your shoes."

Variation

This assignment has typically been given to first-year students in college or younger leaders. Encourage students to seek out and praise a person older than a second-year college student (or someone with a greater level of experience).

Have the acknowledgment, recognition, or encouragement e-mailed blindly to the advisor. You can do this to monitor that the assignment has been done, but also to help a student understand the components of genuine and meaningful recognition.

Reflection and Connection to the Model

This activity puts many students out of their comfort zone. While most students are comfortable saying positive things to others, when they have to give praise for performance of some kind, they must observe more closely so they can find an appropriate situation. Then students verbalize the praise in a genuine way so that it means something to the person receiving it. Also, after they have given praise, students are typically surprised at how good it makes them feel. The "praisee" typically responds very positively, which makes both feel good and creates a bond between the two people. Use opportunities when the students are together to discuss this experience through reflection.

Questions for Discussion

- What did this activity feel like?
- Did you feel genuine recognizing someone when you don't see him or her face-to-face?
- How does this approach to recognizing or acknowledging someone differ (e.g., in impact, reaction, or ease of doing so) from the ideas and behaviors specifically associated with Encourage the Heart?
- How can you apply this type of strategy to what we have discussed that Encourage the Heart really is?

Student LPI Behaviors Associated with This Activity

5 "I praise people for a job well done."
10 "I encourage others as they work on activities and programs in our organization."
15 "I express appreciation for the contributions that people make."
20 "I make it a point to publicly recognize people who show commitment to shared values."

ACTIVITY: IDENTIFYING INDIVIDUAL RECOGNITION TACTICS

Submitted by Amy Pehrson

Objectives

Students will be able to:

- Identify multiple followers whom they would like to recognize for their contributions to the group or organization
- Formulate meaningful and genuine ways of recognizing identified followers
- Follow through on an intentional plan that helps them better recognize others

Number of Participants

- Any size group

Time Required

- 15 to 20 minutes

Materials and Equipment

- Identifying Individual Recognition Tactics worksheet for each student
- Writing tools

Area Setup

- No special setup needed

Facilitator Cue: The worksheet should be used after explaining or teaching the Encourage the Heart practice. This is an activity that can be started, shared with the group, and given as a homework assignment. It can also be followed up on at a later date.

Process

1. After reviewing or teaching the material for Encourage the Heart, give the Identifying Individual Recognition Tactics worksheet to each student.

2. Review the directions on the student worksheet so that the participants understand that they will first fill out the chart at the end of the worksheet; when that is completed, they will complete the Next Steps section.
3. Students begin filling in the columns on the worksheet chart and then complete the Next Steps section.
4. To debrief, consider asking the following questions:
   - Looking at your chart, what do you notice?
   - Which columns were more difficult for you to fill in?
   - Share with the group some of the good or interesting ideas that you came up with.
   - If you have some "I don't knows" in the fourth column, why is that? How will you rectify that?
   - Truthfully, how likely will you be to actually follow through with your ideas for recognizing these people? Why or why not is that?
   - How can you be held accountable to following through on these activities?

Reflection and Connection to the Model

This activity connects to the commitment of recognizing contributions of the practice of Encourage the Heart. It will help participants identify meaningful and individual ways of recognition and also of making the connection to the values, mission, or vision of your organization. Through this activity, a leader is developing relationships with his or her followers and also developing those people with whom he or she works.

Student LPI Behaviors Associated with This Activity

5 "I praise people for a job well done."
10 "I encourage others as they work on activities and programs."
15 "I express appreciation for the contributions that people make."
20 "I make it a point to publicly recognize people who show commitment to shared values."
25 "I find ways for us to celebrate accomplishments."
30 "I make sure that people are creatively recognized for their contributions."

STUDENT WORKSHEET: IDENTIFYING INDIVIDUAL RECOGNITION TACTICS

Directions

1. Identify four people you work with who have succeeded at or accomplished something recently. Write their name in the first column of the chart on this worksheet.
2. Describe the event or activity in the second column.
3. In the third column, identify what portion or area of your group or organization's core value)or mission or vision did this activity address?
4. Based on your personal knowledge of this person, how would he or she like to be recognized for this success or accomplishment? For example, would a gift card be perfect or some token be just right? How about a sign on the group's bulletin board or a note of recognition in the group's newsletter or the student newspaper? Write down ideas that you have that would fit for this person in the fourth column.
5. If your answer to column 4 is, "I don't know," then in the fifth column, write down some ideas of how you could figure this out. How can you get to know the person better to find out? Is there someone in your group who knows this person well whom you could ask? Could you ask that person some sleuth-like questions?
6. When you have filled in the chart, complete the Next Steps section.
7. Find an opportunity to Encourage the Heart of the person you selected, and then do it!
8. Reflect on how the tactic went. Were you successful? Did your recognition make a difference to that person?
9. Which person will you focus on next?

Next Steps

Pick one person from the chart:

1. What is the first step you will do to move forward on encouraging the heart of this person?

2. By when will you have completed this step?

3. By when will you have actually done the suggested tactic?

Identifying Individual Recognition Tactics

Name of person	What will you recognize him or her for?	Which area of your organization's core values or vision or mission did this activity address?	How does this person like to be recognized?	If the answer to "how" is, "I don't know," how will you figure it out?

ACTIVITY: ENCOURAGE THE HEART PARTY TIME WITH YOUR GROUP

Submitted by Erica Lara

Objectives

Students will be able to:

- Appreciate the importance of Encourage the Heart
- See the value and benefit in recognizing contributions
- Show how groups celebrate victories
- Connect celebrations to group values
- See different examples of encouraging others

Number of Participants

- Any size group. Students do part of the activity prior to the party and work in smaller groups of 5 or fewer. If possible, have the small groups consist of members of the same club, team, or other type of group. If not, see the Process instructions on how members can develop their videos to recognize a group's work.

Time Required

- 40 to 60 minutes, which depends on how many 3-minute video clips you will be showing (allow at least 5 minutes per video clip to include transition time and reactions),
- You can shorten or lengthen this activity depending on how long you want the party and debriefing to go.

Materials and Equipment

- Music
- Party decorations
- Cake (optional)
- Computer and projector with a projection screen
- The equipment and materials to shoot a short video; typically a smart phone can work fine

Area Setup

- Set up the room so it looks as if you're having a party; use streamers, balloons, and music.

Facilitator Cue: Students should have read the chapters on Encourage the Heart in *The Student Leadership Challenge*.

Process

At Least a Week before the Class or Session

1. Create groups and, if possible, assign students to them on the basis of their membership in the same club, team, or other type of group. If your audience consists of students who do not come from the same group, give them a specific student group on campus to use for their project. The students' project is to create a 3-minute video that will Encourage the Heart of their own or an assigned particular student group.

Facilitator Cue: Emphasize both recognizing contributions and celebrating values and victories. Challenge students to look not just for good things a group has done, but to learn and understand the group's values (or emphasize their own group's values) and connect the recognition to the group's success in living out their values through their work and activities.

A recommendation is to assign participants in the activity to student groups that could be present when the videos are shown (if they don't already represent the group). If the students of the groups that are being encouraged in the videos aren't normally present in your class or session, invite them to the "party" so they can participate in the celebration.

At the Party

1. Make sure that the students come prepared with their videos on a thumb drive so that they can be set up quickly in class.
2. Start preparations for the party before the students arrive, giving yourself enough time to decorate the room (or have students in the group decorate in advance). Be creative to make the room different from the way it usually does, so that when students walk in, they will feel special.
3. During your preparation, make sure you turn the computer and projector on.
4. Have upbeat music playing when students start to arrive.
5. Let students settle in and mingle when they arrive before starting the activity. During this mingling time, ask students to bring you their thumb drives with their videos and upload the videos so they are ready to play.
6. Stop the music, and review the idea of Encourage the Heart (which students previously read about).

7. Hand out cake or snacks during the video viewing party.
8. Set aside a time at the end of the videos to debrief the reactions.

Facilitator Cue: Have fun! The objective is for your students to walk out of that class or session feeling appreciated and encouraged and having a collective sense and appreciation that their group is doing its work and accomplishing things that are in line with the group's values. They should walk out of that room feeling "lighter." The more that students in the class or workshop can play a role in designing the party, preparing for it, and executing it, the better. If possible, the group should (1) make sure that members who couldn't attend the party are able to at least see the video about their group at a later meeting and (2) find ways to keep the celebration going for the group by continuing the message of celebrating their values and accomplishments. There doesn't need to be a video, but they should come up with ways to have regular celebrations that keep the party going throughout the year.

Reflection and Connection to the Model

The most effective leaders make a habit of looking for what people are doing that is in line with the group's vision and the values. When they see those things being done, they acknowledge them, pointing them out to others as an example of what "we" are all about. This activity helps students have the experience of deliberately looking for ways to acknowledge and recognize others.

Before the party concludes, ask the groups that were recognized if they have any reactions to having their efforts or contributions recognized publicly and creatively by their classmates (peers).

Facilitator Cue: Although the purpose of this suggestion is not for the students who created the videos to get recognition, it does help reinforce the idea that Encourage the Heart has a huge impact on those individuals and the groups who receive it.

After the party or at a subsequent gathering of the students you're teaching soon afterward, discuss the overall experience:

- What was the experience like of trying to identify a group and then looking for contributions the group was making?
  - Was it difficult to find things for which to recognize your chosen group?
  - What specifically did you do to identify those things?
  - How did looking for how the group accomplished its work and achieved success align with the group's values

- Describe the process in developing your video. How did you decide to recognize your group?
  - What were your challenges in developing the message in your video?
  - What specific things were you looking for when determining what to recognize the group for? How are these things related to effective leadership?
- As you think about Encourage the Heart, what did you learn from this exercise that you could apply to the everyday encouragement and celebration of others and of the group?
- While you can't make a video each time you want to give recognition, what can you do on a regular basis that aligns with this practice?

Facilitator Cue: This activity is good to revisit later in your class or program without the video assignment component. In other words, look for the opportunities your students take to Encourage the Heart on their own as a result of this structured assignment.

Student LPI Behaviors Associated with This Activity

5 "I praise people for a job well done."
10 "I encourage others as they work on activities and programs."
15 "I express appreciation for the contributions that people make."
20 "I make it a point to publicly recognize people who show commitment to shared values."
25 "I find ways for us to celebrate accomplishments."
30 "I make sure that people are creatively recognized for their contributions."

• • •

ACTIVITY: RECOGNITION CAR WASH

Submitted by Stephanie Howeth

Objectives

Students will be able to:

- Personally Encourage the Heart of their peers through thanks and recognition
- Understand the difference between compliments and meaningful recognition
- Experience simple but important ways of providing recognition and appreciation

Number of Participants

- Any size group; if possible, form students into an even number of groups of 12 to 16 each

Time Required

- Approximately 20 to 30 minutes, depending on the size of the group (allow 2 to 3 minutes per student within each group).

Materials

- None needed

Area Setup

- An open space large enough for multiple groups to form two facing lines and have space to move

Facilitator Cue: This activity works best with a group that has already formed strong relationships, but it can also work with newly formed groups to promote a sense of community and encouragement. This activity is a fine ending to the close of a program or retreat experience.

Process

1. Have students line up in two parallel rows across from each other. There should be just enough room between the rows for someone to comfortably pass through (as if they were walking through a car wash).
2. Choose one person to be the first "car" to pass through the car wash. That person closes his or her eyes and begins slowly walking.
3. As the student walks, the students in the line will take turns whispering encouragement and recognition to the person. Challenge students to provide encouragement that is genuine and meaningful as opposed to being simply complimentary—for example, "You're a team player who works hard to include everyone" instead of, "You're a nice person." If group members are already comfortable with one another, you might have them share their recognition aloud rather than whisper.
4. When the student passing through the "car wash" has gone through the entire line, he or she steps into position at the end of the line to encourage the other students coming through the car wash.
5. The next student begins the journey through the car wash. Continue until all students have had their chance to go through the car wash.

Facilitator Cue: Keeping groups as even as possible allows the groups to finish at about the same time. Creating more but smaller groups will make this activity run faster if you have time constraints (though it also limits the amount of recognition each student experiences).

Reflection and Connection to the Model

Leaders know that simple compliments are not enough to have the lasting impact to keep people feeling encouraged during times of stress. Acknowledgments need to be specific, be tied to the vision and values of the group, and be genuine so they create a source people can draw on during tough times. This activity helps students think about the specifics of an acknowledgment, how to be clear about the contributions the person has made, and how to articulate it in a way that will have that lasting impact.

Questions for Discussion

- How did it feel to be personally recognized, thanked, and encouraged by your peers?
- If you feel comfortable sharing, what are a few examples of encouragement you received that were particularly meaningful to you?
- What challenges did you have in finding things to tell your peers that were encouraging? What do you think it takes for leaders to find things they can recognize others for?
- What are some of the differences between very simple but important recognition and the traditional types of recognition to which you might be accustomed?
- What type of recognition can have the greatest impact on someone?

Student LPI Behaviors Associated with This Activity

5 "I praise people for a job well done."
15 "I express appreciation for the contributions that people make."
20 "I make it a point to publicly recognize people who show commitment to shared values."
30 "I make sure that people are creatively recognized for their contributions."

• • •

ACTIVITY: RECOGNITION SPEED DATING

Submitted by Clint Whitson

Objectives

Students will be able to:

- Recall the major components of personality type covered by the Myers-Briggs Type Indicator (MBTI) or some other personality type research

- Identify "recognizing others by showing appreciation for individual excellence" and "personalizing recognition" as major components of Encourage the Heart
- Make specific connections between an individual's perceived personality type and specific forms of recognition that are likely to be meaningful and genuine

Number of Participants

- Best with a group of no more than 20 students per facilitator (4 to 8 volunteers and 12 to 16 observers)

Time Required

- 15 minutes with 10 students; 20 to 25 minutes with more than 10 students

Materials and Equipment

- Paper and pen for each participant to capture ideas when brainstorming. Note, however, that this activity is designed for use with the results of a previously administered assessment instrument of some sort, such as the MBTI or other personality inventory.

Area Setup

- 4 tables placed in a row, far enough apart so conversations don't interfere with each other, with two chairs at each table. Seating needed for 12 to 16 observers.

Facilitator Cue: It is not necessary to use observers for this activity. All students can participate in the speed recognition. The purpose of the observers is to point out things that actively involved students might not be aware of as they talk about recognition related to their personality types.

Process

Facilitator Cue: The students must have some knowledge of personality type, and it is recommended that they have completed and debriefed a personality assessment before conducting the activity.

1. Ask for up to 8 student volunteers who have dominant personality characteristics from the MBTI (or their personality assessment)—for example, one person who scored higher on the "I, Introvert" and one who scored higher on the "E, Extravert," or ask for a volunteer to represent any characteristics that might not have been a dominant one.

2. Pair up the volunteers at tables so that each is sitting with someone who does not represent the opposite personality (e.g., an "extravert" and "introvert" of the MBTI should *not* be paired together).
3. Ask each pair to spend exactly 60 seconds together to brainstorm the types of recognition that they believe someone of the personality characteristic they have or represent might find effective.

Facilitator Cue: This is the speed part of the activity so the timing should be as accurate as possible for brainstorming all the different types of recognition that would be meaningful for someone with their combined personality type. *Example*: If "extravert" and "feeling" were matched up together, one possible form of genuine recognition would be to place that person's name or picture on a wall of fame and ask others to write encouraging or kind notes next to the person's picture or name. This could be effective because the individual described most likely enjoys being around other people and cares about the thoughts and feelings of others.

4. Ask each pair to speak at regular volume level so that the observers can hear the conversations happening.
5. After 60 seconds, ask one person from each pair to move one person to the right or left. Again, ideally, the volunteers should not be sitting with someone who represents the opposite of their personality characteristic.
6. Ask the new pairs to now take 60 seconds to brainstorm the different types of recognition for someone with their personality characteristics.
7. This should happen enough times so that all (or most, if there are many characteristics in the assessment you choose) possible matches have taken place.
8. Once the "speed dating" has ended, ask the participants, and then the observers, to talk a little about the process they just experienced and to tell the group the ideas they came up with. Consider using the following questions.

Questions for Participants

- Tell us a little about the process of brainstorming so quickly.
- What were some of the ideas for recognition you came up with that you felt were worth capturing? How did this process feel (having to provide recognition very quickly)? Was it easy or difficult? Why?
- Were there things you knew about the person you were recognizing that helped you determine what (and how) to say something?
- In this short period of time, how did you make your recognition of the other person meaningful?
- Talk about how knowing something more about a person (i.e., his or her personality type and preferences) helps leaders better and more meaningfully recognize others.

- How can you apply what you learned in this activity with how you can recognize others on a more frequent basis?

If observers were used, engage them to discuss their thoughts and feelings about the activity:

Questions for Observers

- What did you observe?
- What did you hear the participants talking about related to the choices they were making and the types of recognitions they were considering?
- What did you see taking place?

Reflection and Connection to the Model

The two pieces of Encourage the Heart that this activity most closely connects with are recognizing others for their individual excellence and personalizing recognition so that it is both genuine and meaningful. Drive home the point that for recognition to be effective, it needs to be meaningful, and for it to be meaningful, you must have some sense of that person's personality, likes and dislikes, and so on. This activity helps students connect what they perceive to be someone's personality type or personality characteristics with a form of recognition that closely aligns with those personality characteristics.

Student LPI Behaviors Associated with This Activity

5 "I praise people for a job well done."
15 "I express appreciation for the contributions that people make."
25 "I find ways for us to celebrate accomplishments."
30 "I make sure people are creatively recognized for their contributions."

• • •

ACTIVITY: GOOD VIBRATIONS

Submitted by Denise M. Peterson

Objectives

Students will be able to:

- Recognize the positive qualities of others as they lead
- Foster an environment in which recognition can happen

- Reflect on their positive actions
- Learn how individual contributions also add to group celebrations of victories and accomplishments

Number of Participants

- Any size group that has some experience together

Time Required

- 15 to 20 minutes for a group of about ten people

Facilitator Cue: The activity relies on people providing feedback to individuals with whom they have worked together to achieve a goal. When participants are from the same group, the activity also helps the group celebrate its accomplishments.

Materials and Equipment

- Construction paper
- Markers or colored pencils
- Tape for posting on a wall if space allows

Area Setup

- Tables to write on or a wall to display the individual sheets.
- Space to move about

Facilitator Cue: This is a good activity to end with when discussing recognition. This activity can be conducted to recognize individuals or celebrate group accomplishments based on the Process instructions you follow (Individual Recognition or Group Recognition).

Process

1. Pass out construction paper and markers to all students.
2. Have students decorate their paper. They at least need to include their name. Some people really go all out and decorate. Give them about 5 minutes to do this.
3. For the next 10 to 12 minutes, depending on the size of the group, have students give individual and group recognition:

- *Individual recognition:* Put the individual sheets on a wall or large table like a gallery. Have students move around so they can add a comment on every sheet that is owned by someone they have worked with.
- *Group recognition:* Either in addition to or in place of individual recognition (if participants are from the same group or represent various groups with enough members from each group present), have students provide comments that acknowledge the group's accomplishments for the year (or other defined time period) following the group instructions.

4. When you invite students to provide comments, which should take 10 to 12 minutes depending on the size of the group, remind them of the purpose of the activity:
    - *Individual recognition:* "Find individuals you wish to provide with a positive statement of your leadership or group experience with them and leave them a message on their paper. Keep moving around to write on people's papers. Remember that the feedback you write has to incorporate some aspect or element of your experience together. For example, "You have a nice smile," doesn't provide information about your experience unless that has relevance to the contribution the person makes (and you [the student] need to make that connection)."

Facilitator Cue: Simplistic types of acknowledgment like, "You have a nice smile," really isn't Encourage the Heart. It is simply a compliment. However, younger students might confuse the two, so you might use this as an example to help students expand their understanding of the difference between compliments and Encourage the Heart. If you are working with older students, challenge them to be thinking of how the feedback has relevance to the contribution one makes.

- *Group recognition:* Using the same spirit and process as with recognizing individuals, students should direct the statements they write to what the group has accomplished. Encourage students to think about what the group has achieved in relation to its goals and vision. How has the group lived out its values? When has the group done great things that used the strengths of its individual members? How has the group overcome obstacles and challenges? What small wins has the group accumulated? Get students to think in terms of the collective success the group has had and how they see that as a member of the group, how they are affected by that as an individual group member, and how the group has changed or grown because of its success.

5. Allow participants time to read through the comments.
6. Consider asking some or all of the following questions to debrief:
    - How do you feel about yourself right now?

Facilitator Cue: Ask both from the perspective of when students gave feedback and when they received their feedback.

- What do the comments you received tell you about your abilities to lead and work with groups? How have individuals' abilities contributed to the group's success?
- What does this tell you about yourself?
- When you gave someone feedback, what types of things did you recall about them that led you to what you wrote or expressed?
- How did you identify the things that you commented about related to the group as a whole?
- How does identifying those things relate to what you need to look for in recognizing others?

Facilitator Cue: For *individual recognition*, ask students to respond to the last question in step 6: "How does identifying those things relate to what you need to look for in recognizing others?" from the perspective of when they know someone well or fairly well and when they might not know the person very well. This is an opportunity to teach how important it is for leaders to get to know those with whom they are working and leading so they might give more relevant recognition.

For *group recognition*, have the group think about how they can take the collection of comments by the individual members and keep them a part of the ongoing conversation the group has about their work. In other words, discuss how the group can continue to do the things they now have recognized and celebrated.

- Is it easy to give meaningful positive feedback, or did you have some individuals for whom comments did not come easily?
- What things are missing when you look at what the group is celebrating? Are there values that were not lived up to? Were there things that happened or that took up a significant amount of time and resources that didn't help the group move toward or achieve its vision? How can the group take steps in the future to address these shortfalls so that next time there can be more to celebrate?

Reflection and Connection to the Model

You can connect this activity to Encourage the Heart by identifying how it is that that as students move into other leadership roles or groups, they take their previous experiences with them (i.e., their "baggage"). If students leave a group knowing their positive contributions to the overall experience, they can incorporate those behaviors into their next experience. This activity allows people to recognize contributions and celebrate the values and victories by individually providing feedback (recognition) and allowing all to see the big picture that making extraordinary things happen comes down to encouraging everyone's participation. At the same time, this can hold true for the group. If members of the group can more clearly see that through their celebrations, the group is making progress toward its vision and living out its values through their actions, behaviors, and collective decisions, then they can finder greater cause to celebrate.

Student LPI Behaviors Associated with This Activity

5 "I praise people for a job well done."
15 "I express appreciation for the contributions that people make."
20 "I make it a point to publicly recognize people who show commitment to shared values."
25 "I find ways for us to celebrate accomplishments."
30 "I make sure that people are creatively recognized for their contributions."

• • •

ACTIVITY: WEB OF YARN

Submitted by Monique Parks

Objectives

Students will be able to:

- Celebrate the community that forms as a result of an accomplishment (or event, achievement, or something else)
- Celebrate what the group has accomplished as a collective whole
- Enforce good feelings and invoke a sense of friendship and camaraderie among a group of leaders
- Experience the effect that genuine and meaningful recognition can have on someone

Number of Participants

- Any size group

Time Required

- Calculate the activity to last about 1 minute per person with about 5 to 10 minutes to begin and conclude (reflect on) the activity

Materials and Equipment

- One ball of string or yarn that is large enough so it can be passed back and forth; it is better to have way too much than to run out

Area Setup

- A space large enough so all group members can stand in a circle

Facilitator Cue: This is a good closing activity for a group at the end of a retreat, training session, major accomplishment, or event the students just put on. It not only recognizes and celebrates the individual student; the collective message is also about celebrating the work of the group (when the students are from the same group or community). Look for messages that students share about each other that are also reflective of the achievements of the group and how the group has realized its vision, lived its values, overcome obstacle and challenges, and become stronger as a result of the individual contributions.

Process

1. Have students form a circle that is as round as possible, with students spaced evenly
2. The first person holds on to the end of a ball of yarn and tosses the ball to another student without letting go of the end of the yarn.
3. When the student catches the ball of yarn, the first person must then say something that the person has contributed, why the contribution made a difference, and what he or she appreciated about the contribution of the person the ball was tossed to. For example, if Alicia tosses the ball to Andrew, she might say, "Andrew is a great researcher. Because of the work he did studying and looking for better prices and giveaways for our event, we were able to not only save money, but the other students are still talking about how cool the miniature mascots were that we gave out."

Facilitator Cue: It is important in this activity for the students to tell what the person contributed, why the contribution made a difference, and the meaning of the appreciation for the contribution. Also, have students make a connection between the individual's contribution and what that did to help the group.

4. Andrew tosses the ball to another person while holding a strand of the yarn and encourages that person in the same manner.
5. The process continues until everyone in the group has had a chance to catch the ball and say something about someone else (the ball should return to the first person to complete the web).
6. By the end, the group will have created a giant web.
7. Have everyone in the circle continue to hold the yarn at their point and tighten up the slack in the yarn to create a tighter web.
8. At this point, the advisor or another person in the group may wish to make closing comments around the experience they just had (what they heard and saw) or the event they used this activity to complete.

Reflection and Connection to the Model

Once everyone has had a chance to catch the ball and receive encouragement, the facilitator should explain that the only way a team can fall apart and fail is if someone is not supporting one of the members. Although this is a closing activity, you may not want to lead an in-depth discussion, but certainly feel free to illustrate the value and importance of Encourage the Heart and use what the students experienced to show how genuine and meaningful recognition can make others feel stronger. Individual contributions are important. Share your observations of them as they collectively influenced the group's accomplishments. Better yet, have the group share how they thought the things that were shared by each person become a way for the group to celebrate what it has accomplished. In other words, have students share how they see the group living out its values and realizing or coming closer to its vision.

As you can see by the individual contributions and the impact on the group that you've just discussed, you can relate specific comments to the idea of teamwork. Leaders and group members need to work together and not let others down. If one person in the circle dropped his or her strand of yarn, that would demonstrate to students how the web weakens if the whole group is not working together. This can also be compared to trying to untangle the strong web of yarn the group has just created.

This activity is connected to Encourage the Heart because of the way in which each person recognizes another. It allows the group to encourage one another by creating a general sense of strengthening others. This activity helps to recognize contributions by showing appreciation for individuals' excellence and creates a spirit of community. It also allows others to praise people, provide support, publicly celebrate accomplishments, and creatively recognize people in a genuine and meaningful way. At the end of this activity, the leaders should celebrate together for their contribution to making the group a success.

Student LPI Behaviors Associated with This Activity

15 "I express appreciation for the contributions that people make."

20 "I make it a point to publicly recognize people who show commitment to shared values."

25 "I find ways for us to celebrate accomplishments."

30 "I make sure that people are creatively recognized for their contributions."

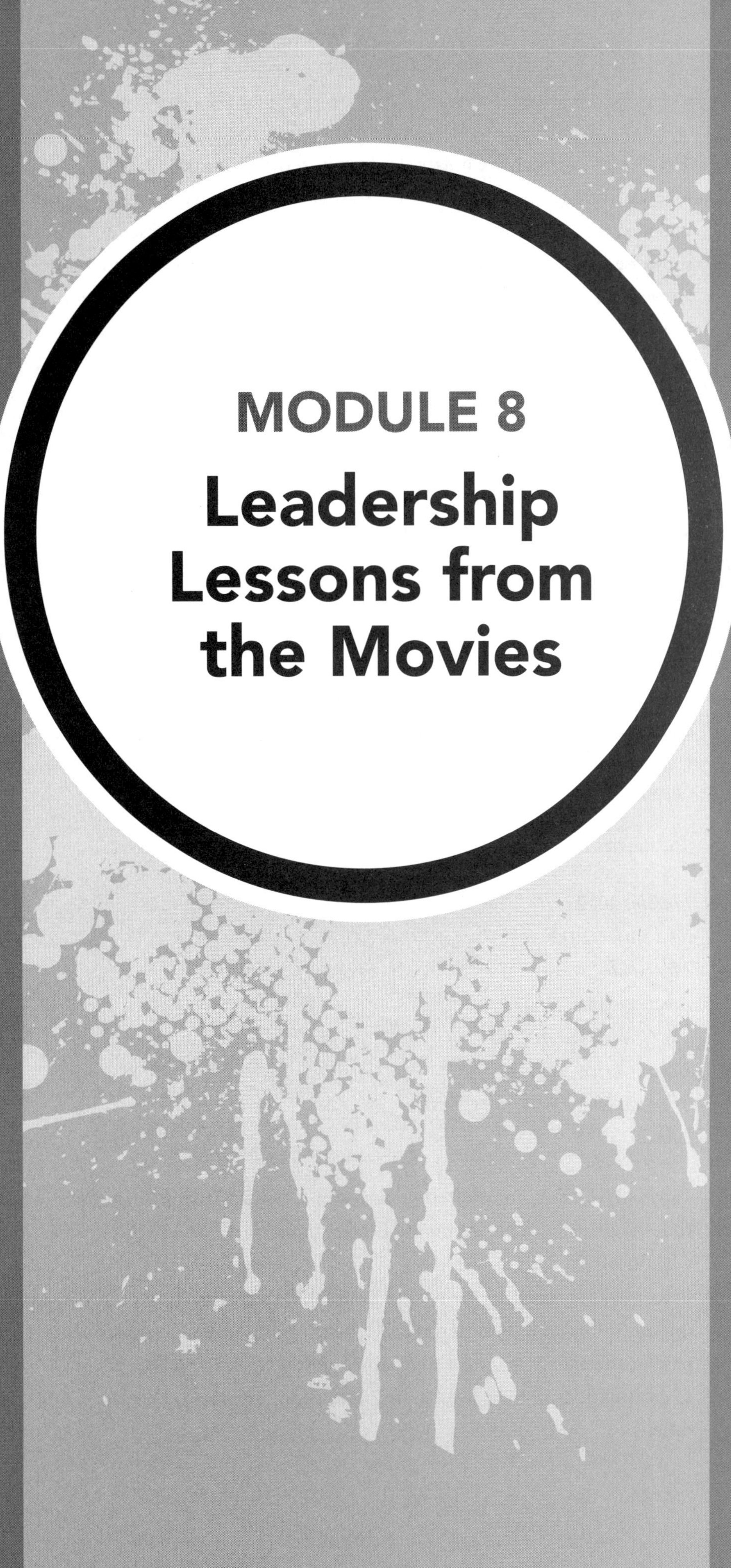

MODULE 8

Leadership Lessons from the Movies

The Five Practices of Exemplary Leadership show up in many movies. The activities that follow feature selected movies and clips that illustrate the practices in a number of ways. Included for each activity is a brief synopsis of the movie, a description of the clips that showcase a particular practice or practices, and then a series of questions for students to answer or consider. While these movies are not exhaustive of the many that you can use to teach The Five Practices, they were chosen for their potential appeal to young leaders, the strength of the messages they contain to demonstrate leadership, and the direct impact they can have in your teaching without consuming a great deal of time to view the movies. Many movies have even greater value if you are able to incorporate the entire film into your teaching.

Movies are a great way to spark creative thinking about how The Five Practices show up in real (or even imagined) life. While the clips listed here are clear examples of the noted practices, look for examples of other practices or leadership behaviors not mentioned in the activity or that are illustrated elsewhere in the selected films.

ACTIVITIES

Submitted by Gary Morgan

The movies are listed in chronological order by the most recent release date:

Lincoln, 2012
Soul Surfer, 2011
Moneyball, 2011
Amazing Grace, 2007
The Great Debaters, 2007
Coach Carter, 2005
The Lion King, 1994
Gandhi, 1985

Many of these movies contain examples of leadership in unique, very difficult times and in unusual situations. Leadership is not just for those times, but that is when it often emerges. We know that the leadership behaviors that make up The Five Practices are needed in many situations, sometimes the very dramatic and often the uneventful but not unimportant. We urge you to challenge the students who participate in the activities in this book to earnestly work to apply what they have learned to all situations in their lives, simple and complex, where their leadership can make a difference.

MOVIE: *LINCOLN*

2012. Director: Steven Spielberg
Screenplay: Tony Kushner
Distribution: Touchtone Pictures, 20th Century Fox
Rated PG-13 for scenes of war violence, carnage, and brief strong language (noted in selected scenes)

The Five Practices Exhibited in the Selected Scenes of *Lincoln*

- Model the Way
- Inspire a Shared Vision
- Challenge the Process
- Enable Others to Act

Abraham Lincoln's second term sees his struggle to get the US House of Representatives to pass the Thirteenth Amendment, to abolish slavery, to the US Constitution.

Synopsis

Abraham Lincoln, sixteenth president of the United States, struggles to deal with a divided nation. The Civil War is in its fourth year, and the issue of slavery dominates the House of Representatives as Lincoln enters his second term. This film focuses on the work and challenges that Lincoln and his advisors face in trying to get a new amendment to the Constitution ratified. The amendment passed the Senate the previous year and Lincoln balances the potential to end the war peacefully with his commitment to abolishing slavery.

Scene Descriptions

Facilitator Cue: You might find value in having students view the entire movie. This would be appropriate for program structures such as a class or an ongoing leadership workshop series where you can show the movie in one of your sessions or have students view the movie on their own time and be prepared to discuss in the leadership session. There are many leadership lessons and examples of The Five Practices, plus other valuable leadership lessons, in other shorter scenes throughout the movie. In fact we found no fewer than eighteen leadership lessons in the movie. You are likely to find even more.

The following scene descriptions illustrate a number of The Five Practices in the film. You can view these scenes as individual clips, stopping for discussion in between, or watch the whole sequence with discussion afterward. You might find value in having students view the entire movie. This would be appropriate for program structures such as a class or an ongoing leadership workshop series where you can show the movie in one of your sessions or have students view the movie on their own time and be prepared to discuss in the leadership session.

- *Chapters 3–6:* "A New Amendment," "War Powers," "The House Debate," and "Getting Out the Vote." Begins in chapter 3 of the DVD at approximately 00:15:37 (0 hours, 15 minutes, 37 seconds) to 00:48:59.

Facilitator Cue: Some short segments in these scenes are unrelated to these lessons. You can consider forwarding from 00:35:11 to 00:40:29, although 00:35:11 to 00:39:11 may provide some insights to views of the representatives and other leaders. Also skip 00:42:13 to 00:44:32.

Facilitator Cue: Strong language between 20:30 and 21:20.

In several scenes within these chapters, Lincoln shares his ideas about why slavery should be abolished, whether related to a military necessity, ending the war altogether, or as a means to establish equal rights. Lincoln is challenged by Secretary of State Seward about the impossibility of getting enough votes to pass the amendment, as well as how to go about getting those votes and even whether pursuing the amendment and votes is the best course of action. There are many instances where Lincoln has opportunities to share his views on the amendment and the importance of passing it, including conversations with his secretary of state, the Jolly family from Missouri who share approval and disapproval for different reasons, his cabinet, representatives of the Republican Party (Lincoln's own political party), conversations with Preston Blair (a prominent journalist, one of the founders of the new Republican Party and an influential supporter of President Lincoln), and others. There are also conversations that don't include Lincoln but favor or disfavor Lincoln's influence.

- *Chapter 10:* "No 16-Year-Olds Left." Begins in chapter 10 of the DVD at approximately 01:14:14 to 01:18:51.

In the middle of the night, Lincoln goes to the communications room, where two soldiers are on duty. From a previous scene, Lincoln has decided to have Confederate commissioners visit Washington, DC, thinking they wanted to discuss a resolution to the war. In a conversation with the soldiers, Lincoln uses a mathematical theory of Euclid that basically states, "Things that are equal to the same thing are also equal to each other." As Lincoln describes this theory to the soldiers, he becomes clearer about the decision he needs to make. As a result, he changes his telegram to have the Confederates stay until they are summoned to Washington.

- *Chapter 11:* "Equality under the Law." Begins in chapter 11 of the DVD at approximately 01:18:55 to 01:24:30.

A challenge to Representative Thaddeus Stevens arises in the House of Representatives when he is challenged by an opposing representative (Mr. Wood) to express his "true" beliefs on the purpose of the Thirteenth Amendment. Stevens recognizes that his opponents are trying to coerce a response from him that might show his true views and, more important, create an opportunity for public backlash by framing the amendment in an even more popular light. Stevens is confronted outside the hall by one of his allies about why he didn't state his "true" understanding of the amendment.

Facilitator Cue: You might also show chapter 8 ("The Grand Reception," 00:55:28 to 00:58:50) to watch Lincoln discuss with Stevens how he might temper his demands and arguments with Congress so that the amendment might pass. In this scene, you will see more of Stevens's beliefs about the amendment and be able to compare this view with the one he shares in chapter 11.

- *Chapters 13–14:* "Bipartisan Support" and "Fairness and Freedom." Begins in chapter 13 and continues into chapter 14 of the DVD at approximately 01:36:01 to 01:46:40. There is some strong language in these scenes.

Several examples of leadership behaviors are evident in these scenes. The president visits men who have been working behind the scenes to procure votes in favor of the amendment. From this visit, three opposing legislators are met with attempts to change their votes. Next, Lincoln meets with his advisors, who continue to press him to take the path of a peaceful negotiation. Lincoln passionately counters with yet another vision for freedom and challenges these leaders to get the remaining votes to pass the amendment.

Leadership Lessons from *Lincoln*

Discussion Questions for "A New Amendment," "War Powers," "The House Debate," and "Getting Out the Vote"

1. What various viewpoints do you hear from the many politicians about why or how slavery should (or should not) be abolished and how the war could be ended with abolition or directly through peaceful negotiations? How does Lincoln respond or react to these various perspectives from representatives of his own party, his cabinet, and others from whom he seeks support?
2. Where are opportunities directly or indirectly provided or encouraged by Lincoln for the various parties to accomplish Lincoln's goals and vision for abolishing slavery?

Where and how do you see other leaders in the scenes also directly or indirectly encouraging opportunities for others to do their work?

3. How does influence play into the scenarios you see throughout the scenes? What is a leader's role or responsibility to influence, and how does that behavior from a leader have an impact on others?

Discussion Questions for "Equality under the Law"

1. Representative Stevens has strong beliefs about the equality of all men. In this scene, he is challenged by one of his contemporaries. At the beginning of the scene, when Stevens is on the House floor, what do you hear in his reply about the purpose of the amendment? Does his answer change at any point in his multiple answers?
2. When Stevens is confronted in the hall after the floor sessions, what do you hear in his response to his colleague? Did you hear anything different from what he said on the floor?
3. You've seen an articulation of Stevens's values in both cases. Did he represent his values in light of his desire to get the amendment passed?
   - How do or how can leaders accomplish what is important to them while not compromising their values? Do you think Stevens compromised his, or did he express them in a way that accomplished his purpose?

> *Facilitator Cue:* "Equality under the Law" provides a great example of how leaders find ways to accommodate others' views and challenge their positions while still holding true to their own values. In other words, discuss when your students compromise their values versus when they can hold true to their values and find creative ways to influence others.

Discussion Questions for "No 16-Year-Olds Left"

1. What do you hear in Lincoln's conversation with the telegraph soldiers (most likely a conversation with himself) in his deliberation about having the Confederate commissioners come to Washington to supposedly discuss peace?

> *Facilitator Cue:* By discussing a peaceful resolution to the war, Lincoln fears that the Thirteenth Amendment may never pass because he is pushing the passing as a military necessity (its passage is necessary in order for the war to end).

2. How does this transformation of Lincoln's thinking demonstrate his values through his actions?

Facilitator Cue: Obviously Lincoln is strongly opposed to slavery and believes all men are created equal. Therefore, he is exhibiting his value of equality by doing what he believes necessary to end slavery (even if there could be a peaceful resolution to the war yet keeping slavery intact).

Discussion Questions for "Bipartisan Support" and "Fairness and Freedom"

1. In Representative Stevens's conversation with Representative Coffroth, did you see examples of leadership, manipulation, negotiation, compromise, something else, or any combination of these?
   - If you saw leadership, describe what examples you saw. If not, describe the role of a leader in a situation such as this and how leaders should (or could) take a direction in their actions that stray toward or further from effective leadership.
2. Do you see anything similar to or different from Representative Stevens's conversation with Representative Coffroth in the way the president interacts with Representative Yeaman? What does the president appeal to, and is that in line with his vision?
3. When Lincoln visits with his advisors and they realize that he bypassed a conversation with the South for an end to the war in light of ending slavery, what did you hear in his remarks?
   - How did Lincoln inspire his advisors to continue their work in obtain votes to pass the amendment? Aside of another expression of his vision, did you see anything else that he offered up to his advisors?
4. As a leader, how do you enable others to fulfill their responsibilities?

• • •

MOVIE: *SOUL SURFER*

2011. Director: Sean McNamara
Screenplay: Sean McNamara, Deborah Schwartz, Douglas Schwartz, and Michael Berk
Distribution: Tri Star Pictures and Film District
Rated PG for accident sequence (not included in the selected scenes)

The Five Practices Exhibited in the Selected Scenes of *Soul Surfer*

- Model the Way
- Challenge the Process
- Enable Others to Act
- Encourage the Heart

Bethany Hamilton, a teen surfer, loses her arm in a shark attack and then overcomes immense odds to become one of the best teen surfers on the surfing circuit. This film is based on her true story.

Synopsis

A story more about the tragedy a young teen must overcome than her place as a champion surfer in the ocean, this movie tells how Bethany Hamilton matures to understand the challenges of life as a young woman from a family of surfers who wanted to compete on the waves of Hawaii. A tragic accident takes her life on a much different path, where she finds what is really important and comes to realize the impact she can have on others around the world.

Scene Descriptions

The following descriptions for five scenes in the film illustrate a number of The Five Practices. You can view these scenes as individual clips, stopping to discuss them in between, or watch the whole sequence with discussion afterward. You might find value in having students view the entire movie. This would be appropriate for program structures such as a class or an ongoing leadership workshop series where you can show the movie in one of your sessions or have students view the movie on their own time and be prepared to discuss in the leadership session.

> *Facilitator Cue:* There are no chapter titles in this movie.

- *Chapter 3:* Begins in chapter 3 of the DVD at approximately 00:12:46 (0 hours, 12 minutes, 46 seconds) to 00:13:42.

The beach gang gathers for a Rad Night fellowship headed by a youth leader who challenges them to begin to look at things in their lives differently than they might have had in the past.

- *Chapter 11:* Begins in chapter 11 of the DVD at approximately 01:00:34 to 01:01:13.

Bethany participates in her first surfing competition since the shark attack. Because of the time it takes her to paddle out to the wave, the competition committee has awarded her extra time to swim out to the waves.

- *Chapter 13:* Begins in chapter 13 of the DVD at approximately 01:15:05 to 01:18:26.

Facilitator Cue: This scene includes religious references.

Facilitator Cue: You may wish to begin this scene at the 01:12:34 mark to offer an additional perspective on how conditions can affect one's reactions to certain circumstances and challenge leaders to continue to work to gain a different perspective.

Bethany takes a break from surfing and makes a trip to Thailand with a youth group to help with the aftermath of the tsunami that devastated that country. As the group helps people near the coastline, Bethany befriends a little boy who is without his family. She persuades him to get into the water and gives him a little surfing lesson.

- *Chapter 13:* Continues in chapter 13 of the DVD at approximately 01:18:26 to 01:20:14.

Facilitator Cue: While this segment continues directly after the previous one, we suggest you pause and discuss the first scenes in chapter 13.

Bethany returns from Thailand to find hundreds of letters from fans around the world. These letters move her because of the inspiration and courage they say she has given others to meet their challenges and obstacles head on.

- *Chapter 16:* Begins in chapter 16 of the DVD at approximately 01:38:18 to 01:39:38.

Bethany finishes the national surfing championships in fifth place. Afterward she is interviewed by the media and expresses the appreciation she has for the opportunities as well as the challenges she has faced. She recognizes the influence she can have on others by sharing her experiences.

Leadership Lessons from *Soul Surfer*

Discussion Questions for Chapter 3

1. As a leader, how do you try to solve challenges or problems when you get stuck?
    - How would you use the advice given by the group leader when you are working with your groups and trying to resolve or solve a complex issue?

Discussion Questions for Chapter 11

1. Bethany was a champion surfer before the shark attack. How do you think she decides whether to take the extra time the judges allotted her as a head start?
   - How does this play into Bethany's values
   - What influence do you think plays into her decision given that one of her fiercest competitors is next to her when she is made this allowance?
   - As a leader, when you think of character or living out your values, what are the external influences that could affect your choices (whether you stick to your character or values or you stray)?

Discussion Questions for the First Part of Chapter 13

1. How does Bethany enable not only the little boy but others to gain the courage to get back into the water?
2. What behaviors do you see Bethany exhibit that make others take notice and take what typically would be simple steps but that are very difficult for them?

Discussion Questions for the Continuation of Chapter 13

1. What did you see in Bethany's attitude based on the letters and stories she received from Stephanie, Dillon, and Logan?

> *Facilitator Cue:* In the film, both Dillon and Logan are referred to here by name (as well as in chapter 16), although it might be confusing as to which letters Bethany and her mother are talking about since they use different names.

   - How do leaders' attitudes influence the work they do, as well as how others view them?
2. Bethany decides not to give up. As a leader, do you know your own level of commitment to what you are doing?
   - How does your commitment ebb and flow and relate to your doing what you say you will do?
3. Bethany's mom, in response to why so many others were writing to her daughter, said it was because Bethany tried. When do you decide not to try or not to take the chances or risks that leaders need to take?

Discussion Questions for Chapter 16

1. How do Bethany's words about how others might be watching her (Stephanie, Logan, and Dillon) relate to how others watch leaders?
   - What opportunity does Bethany realize she has because of the challenge (now as she views it, an opportunity) she had by losing her arm?

2. What lesson do you learn from Bethany's philosophy here when she talks about anything being possible?

• • •

MOVIE: *MONEYBALL*

2011. Director: Bennet Miller
Screenplay: Steven Zaillian and Aaron Sorkin
Distribution: Columbia Pictures
Rated PG-13 for strong language and occurrences are noted in appropriate scenes

The Five Practices Exhibited in the Selected Scenes of *Moneyball*

- Inspire a Shared Vision
- Challenge the Process
- Enable Others to Act

Moneyball is a movie about the 2002 Oakland Athletics major league baseball team. The film is based on the true story of a general manager who goes against all the traditional ways of running a baseball team.

Synopsis

While *Moneyball* is on the surface a baseball movie, it is really a movie about organizational change, strategy, and finding the real talents that lie within a team's (group's) members. The story is based on the drive of the Oakland A's to win a championship. Billy Beane is considered one of the premier general managers in baseball. He comes by this reputation by a unique system of evaluating the talent of baseball players and recruiting his team differently than has ever been done before. Billy puts his faith in an economics major recently out of college to devise a new way to create a winning team. The effort starts out horribly, but later in the season, The A's win more games in a row than any other team in more than fifty years.

Scene Descriptions

The following descriptions for five scenes in the film illustrate a number of The Five Practices. You can view these scenes as individual clips, stopping to discuss them in between, or watch the whole sequence with discussion afterward. You might find value in having students view the entire movies. This would be appropriate for program structures such as a class or an ongoing leadership workshop series where you can show the movie in one of your sessions, or have students view the movie on their own time and be prepared to discuss in the leadership session.

Facilitator Cue: There are no chapter titles in this movie.

- *Chapter 2:* Begins in chapter 2 of the DVD at approximately 00:08:26 (0 hours, 8 minutes, 26 seconds) to 00:12:37. There is some strong language in this scene.

The scouting and management team meets to try to figure out how they can fill vacant spots on the team due to player trades in the baseball off-season. Billy Beane, the general manager, challenges their thinking about how they select new players.

Facilitator Cue: In addition you can watch chapter 5 at 00:31:24 to 00:36:42 and see some more in-depth discussion about how Billy is going to rethink the way the team selects players. For this segment, look at how the staff interacts with Billy. You can lead a conversation about what, as a leader, he could have done with this group (either before or during the meeting) to be proactive about the group's concern and anger.

- *Chapter 7:* Begins in chapter 7 of the DVD at approximately 00:57:28 to 00:58:38.

Billy meets with the team's manager, Art Howe, to apologize for not bringing Howe in at the very beginning of the conversation where Billy could have shared his vision. They exchange remarks about who should have been played in the game based on Billy's theory.

Facilitator Cue: You might also view a small segment in chapter 8 at 00:59:15 to 00:59:58 to see how critics of Billy's vision respond.

- *Chapter 8:* Begins in chapter 8 of the DVD at approximately 01:00:16 to 01:02:30.

Billy and Peter Brand, the "kid" he hired to help him determine the team's roster, talk about how to handle the players on the team. Billy coaches Peter on how to interact with the players and sends him on the road to represent him.

- *Chapter 10:* Begins in chapter 10 of the DVD at approximately 01:22:14 to 01:25:05.

Billy talks to one of his better players: David Justice. He looks to see what is affecting David's performance and to see how he might get him to better understand his role on the team as an older player. David then goes to have another conversation with one of the uncertain players on the team, first baseman Scott Hatteberg.

- *Chapter 10:* A continuation of chapter 10 of the DVD at approximately 01:25:06 to 01:26:14.

Billy and Peter have conversations with a number of the players about things they can or should be doing specific to their position or role in the game.

Leadership Lessons from *Moneyball*

Discussion Questions for Chapter 2

1. Billy listens and then challenges the staff on what problems they are trying to solve. What do leaders try to do when they face obstacles and challenges?
   - How do leaders help their followers understand what they need to focus on so they can do the best they possibly can in their roles and at their jobs?

Discussion Questions for Chapter 7

1. What in this scene gives you insight into how a leader should define his or her vision?
2. What could a leader do so that others are clear about his or her vision of the group?
   - How does a leader determine who should be included in the process of defining a vision or understanding the vision of the group?

Discussion Questions for Chapter 8

1. What do you see Billy doing with Peter in this conversation?
   - How would you describe Peter's confidence level with understanding player performance versus his confidence in actually relating to and managing the players? What does Billy do to address this?

Discussion Questions for the First Part of Chapter 10

1. What does Billy appeal to in David to help him see a different role he might have with the team?
2. What do you see Billy do at the end of the conversation?
3. How does this conversation translate into leadership behaviors you could have with your individual group members to help them be more effective and successful in what they do?
4. How does David then interact with Scott Hatteberg in the break room? What message do you see him try to convey to Scott?
   - Was he successful? Why or why not?
   - If you were to talk with David after his conversation with Scott, what would you say?

Discussion Questions for the Continuation of Chapter 10

1. What strategies do you see Billy and Peter using with the different players?
2. When the players challenge Billy and Peter's thinking, how do they deal with it?

• • •

MOVIE: *AMAZING GRACE*

2007. Director: Michael Apted
Written by: Steven Knight
Distribution: Momentum Pictures (UK), Samuel Goldwyn Films (US)
Rated PG for thematic content around slavery and mild language

The Five Practices Exhibited in the Selected Scenes of *Amazing Grace*

- Model the Way
- Inspire a Shared Vision
- Challenge the Process
- Enable Others to Act

This movie, set in the late 1700s, is based on a true story of British parliamentarian William Wilberforce who crusaded for the abolition of slavery in England.

Synopsis

William Wilberforce, one of the youngest members ever elected to the House of Commons, spends two decades of his career in Parliament fighting for the cause of abolishing the slave trade in England. He introduces bills over five years, yet even with the growing support of the House as well as the prime minister, none of his bills pass. Eventually he finds a creative way to financially crush the many industries dependent on slave trade through a law that allows their ships to be seized as they traffic slaves from the West Indies and other places to England.

Scene Descriptions

The following descriptions for three scenes in the film illustrate a number of The Five Practices. You can view these scenes as individual clips, stopping to discuss them in between, or watch the whole collective sequence with discussion afterward.

Facilitator Cue: As with the movie *Lincoln*, you might find value in having students view the entire movie because there are many leadership lessons and examples of The Five Practices in much shorter scenes throughout the movie.

- *Chapter 10:* "A Day Like No Other." Begins in chapter 10 of the DVD at approximately 00:49:43 (0 hours, 49 minutes, 43 seconds) to 00:52:37.

This clip shows the vision that William Wilberforce has for what England could be like if slavery were abolished, not to mention his ideas that all men should be free. He implores the House of Commons to pass a bill that will once and for all abolish slavery and create for the rest of the world an example of how the British financial empire will not collapse as a result of the end of the slave trade.

- *Chapter 15:* "Out of the Bottle." Begins in chapter 15 of the DVD at approximately 01:16:10 to 01:18:48. Pick up again at 01:19:17 (or continue on) to 01:19:46.

This section depicts the many challenges and arguments that William faces in Parliament to his bills on abolishing slavery. The connections his opposition make about why Wilberforce isn't fit to be a member of the House as well as why England should not end the slave trade include accusations of William's being a French spy to his having a close relationship with Thomas Jefferson (whom the English despise because of his leadership in the United States). The opposing members of the House propose that William is now against the king because his work to end slavery constitutes seditious acts under the laws of England. The accusations that are now being used by William's opposition create incredible new challenges, legal and otherwise, for William to gain support for his bills.

- *Chapters 20–21:* "A New Strategy" and "Blindsided." Begins in chapter 20 and continues on to chapter 21 of the DVD at approximately 01:31:34 to 01:37:40.

William's support begins to gain momentum as his allies grow in numbers, sparked by the return of James Stephen, an attorney who helped Wilberforce design a legal means to approach abolishing slavery from a different angle. This scene describes how William crafts a new bill that forbids cargo ships (many of which transport slaves to England) from using neutral flags. Because they now fly the flags from where they are registered (many times a form of American flag), the ships and their cargo can be seized. Within a short period of time, this act crushes the slave trafficking industry and puts many businesses that rely on the trade out of business.

Leadership Lessons from *Amazing Grace*

Discussion Questions for "A Day Like No Other"

1. On what occasions in this scene did William Challenge the Process?
2. Describe the vision that William shared as he talked about slavery. What reactions did you see to his vision? Describe the influence you think he had.
3. What first steps did William take? How do those demonstrate any of The Five Practices of Exemplary Leadership?

Discussion Questions for "Out of the Bottle"

1. What obstacles did William now face, based on the House of Commons's new challenges to him, and how did he address them?
2. Thinking about this scene and what William was facing, how can leaders deal with the external forces that may continue to oppose them and their vision or even accuse them of untrue or inaccurate actions or character traits?

Discussion Questions for "A New Strategy" and "Blindsided"

1. How were others encouraged and enabled in the beginning of this scene when the gentlemen talked about the next steps to take?
2. How did you see Challenge the Process exhibited throughout these scenes?

> *Facilitator Cue:* This movie also shows The Five Practices throughout the story in many smaller ways than are depicted in these three scenes. This movie would be a good one to use as an out-of-class or outside-the-workshop "assignment" to have students see how leadership shows up in many ways and places.

• • •

MOVIE: *THE GREAT DEBATERS*

2007. Director: Denzel Washington

Screenplay: Robert Eisele

Distribution: The Weinstein Company

Rated PG-13 for thematic material, including violence and disturbing images, and for language and brief sexuality. Only mild language is briefly included in some of the selected scenes.

The Five Practices Exhibited in the Selected Scenes of *The Great Debaters*

- Inspire a Shared Vision
- Challenge the Process
- Enable Others to Act

This movie is a dramatization based on a true story in the mid-1930s about a small Texas college that rises to a level of national awareness as a result of the first-ever debate between a black college and a white college (Harvard University in the movie).

Synopsis

Professor Melvin Tolson teaches and coaches the debate team at historically black Wiley College, in Marshall, Texas, during the 1930s when race relations in the country, and particularly the South, were at great odds and Jim Crow laws ruled. Tolson assembled a debate team of three men and one woman who would go on to a nearly undefeated season that culminated in beating the national debate champion, Harvard University. (Note the dramatic license of the movie: Wiley College actually debated and defeated the University of Southern California, the national champions at the time.) The film depicts the debate team's trials and tribulations as they ascend to prominence while they deal with the atrocities of racism, daily insults, a lynching, and more.

Scene Descriptions

The following descriptions for five scenes in the film illustrate a number of The Five Practices. You can view these scenes as individual clips, stopping to discuss them in between, or watch the whole sequence with discussion afterward. This would be appropriate for program structures such as a class or an ongoing leadership workshop series where you can show the movie in one of your sessions, or have students view the movie on their own time and be prepared to discuss in the leadership session.

- *Chapter 15:* "Tolson's Arrest." Begins in chapter 15 of the DVD at approximately 01:12:13 (1 hour, 12 minutes, 13 seconds) to 01:14:27.

In this clip we see Professor Tolson unjustly arrested for working with sharecroppers to help them form a union. As a result of this incident, the professor's role at Wiley College begins to change. He is more constrained in how he teaches his students. Yet he is undaunted and finds strength in the defeats he faces. He uses this experience to inspire and encourage his students in their work.

- *Chapters 20–21*: "Travelling to Boston" and "Change of Debate Topic." Begins in chapter 20 and continues through chapter 21 of the DVD at approximately 1:35:38 to 1:39:14.

These scenes deliver a number of unexpected situations that the student debaters must face. First, they learn that their professor won't be allowed to accompany them to Harvard University because of the conditions of his probation. Once they arrive at Harvard and settle in, they receive a note that the topic for their debate, which they had prepared diligently for, has been changed and they have forty-eight hours to develop new arguments. The character Henry Lowe, a student, is not the leader (in charge) of the group and faces some difficult decisions.

Facilitator Cue: You may wish to pause the movie here before going to the next scene and go to the discussion questions for these scenes.

- *Chapters 21–22:* "Sacrifice." Continues on to the beginning of chapter 22 of the DVD at approximately 01:41:01 to 01:43:38.

This brief clip shows how one of the students, James Farmer Jr., comes to realize something about himself and the impact that confidence can have on others.

The debate between Wiley College and Harvard University is on.

- *Chapter 23:* "The Harvard Debate." Begins in chapter 23 of the DVD at approximately 01:43:38 to 01:55:40.

Facilitator Cue: Notice the dialogue at time marks 01:45:22, 01:47:06 and 01:52:48 until the end of the scene.

In the debate, the two teams argue back and forth about the value, or lack thereof, of civil disobedience. The complexity of a debate is evident here and emphasized by the careful scripting of the arguments. Though the dialogue is in the form of a debate, the imagery and emotional appeal stirred up by both arguments on civil disobedience provide descriptive elements of unique and perhaps ideal conclusions.

Leadership Lessons from *The Great Debaters*

Discussion Questions for "Tolson's Arrest"

1. What do you think Professor Tolson is thinking about as a result of his arrest, and how does he use these thoughts to move forward?

2. How does Tolson take his experience and use it to teach, motivate, and encourage his students?
3. How does he use the recent events to Enable Others to Act?

Discussion Questions for "Travelling to Boston" and "Change of Debate Topic"

1. What did you see Professor Tolson do when addressing his students and explaining that he will not be accompanying them to Boston?
   - When unforeseen circumstances arise, what responsibilities do leaders have in addressing them?
2. What type of vision do you see expressed by the students? Is it a shared vision?

> *Facilitator Cue:* If you use the entire movie, you might deepen the question here to have students describe how the vision of Professor Tolson has developed throughout the story to this point.

3. What is Henry Lowe facing now as a leader? What leadership behaviors do you see him exhibit with his peers?
4. How does conflict play into the interactions of the students? How would you deal with these actions as a leader? Do you think they are addressed effectively here?

Discussion Questions for "Change of Debate Topic" (scene with James Farmer Jr.)

1. What is it that appeals to James, and what do you see happening to him as a result?
2. What practice is evident in the scene from James's revelation?

Discussion Questions for "Sacrifice"

1. What do you see here in the script that could represent vision based on how the moderator (the dean of students) introduces the teams?
2. Do you see the introduction of the dean of students as having remnants of any of the other practices?

> *Facilitator Cue:* Have your students think about the journey the students of Wiley College have embarked on and how the dean of students' way of introducing them has the flavor of how they have to Challenge the Process along the way. Their being at Harvard is a result of this practice.

Discussion Questions for "Sacrifice" and "The Harvard Debate"

1. While this scene is in the form of a formal debate, what aspects of vision do you hear and notice?

2. What reactions do you see that might indicate others are finding a shared relationship to the remarks made by the debaters? What do you see differently from the remarks (and reactions) by the Wiley debaters versus the Harvard debaters?

• • •

MOVIE: *COACH CARTER*

2005. Director: Thomas Carter
Screenplay: Mark Schwahn and John Gatins
Distribution: Paramount Pictures
Rated PG-13 for strong language and violence (noted in selected scenes)

The Five Practices Exhibited in the Selected Scenes of *Coach Carter*

- Model the Way
- Inspire a Shared Vision
- Challenge the Process
- Enable Others to Act

A new basketball coach takes on a troubled team at a troubled school and uses unique (and controversial) methods to lead the team and its individual members to success.

Synopsis

Coach Ken Carter takes over a troubled and unsuccessful team at a difficult high school in a rough neighborhood. Being a former basketball player himself at that same high school, he takes personal pride and genuine interest in the team and the school. Carter introduces a "contract" that he requires his players to agree to and sign if they wish to play for him. The contract requires specific behaviors as well as academic standards that are above the required standards for athletes. After meeting significant resistance from first the players, then their parents, and then the community, Carter struggles to overcome obstacles, challenges to the values he tries to instill in the team, and efforts to dismantle his vision for the team.

Scene Descriptions

The following descriptions for three scenes in the film illustrate a number of The Five Practices. You can view these scenes as individual clips, stopping to discuss them in between, or watch the whole sequence with discussion afterward. This would be appropriate for program structures such as a class or an ongoing leadership workshop series where you can show the movie in one of your sessions, or have students view the movie on their own time and be prepared to discuss in the leadership session.

- *Chapter 3:* "Contract." Begins in chapter 3 of the DVD at approximately 00:09:29 (0 hours, 9 minutes, 29 seconds) to 00:13:56.

> *Facilitator Cue:* There is some mild violence and language in this clip

Coach Carter meets his basketball team for the first time as their new coach. His introduction is immediately met with resistance from the team. The coach outlines his expectations for the team and presents them with a contract he tells them they must uphold to not only be successful but to remain members of the team.

- *Chapter 5:* "Student Athlete." Begins in chapter 5 of the DVD at approximately 00:20:11 to 00:21:45.

Carter meets with the parents and their sons about the rules and contract he has put in place for the players. Many of the parents resent his new approach, arguing that this is just a basketball team. Coach responds by describing how basketball is a privilege and how he expects his team players to work to deserve this privilege.

- *Chapter 9:* "Classroom Performance." Begins in chapter 9 of the DVD at approximately 00:48:34 to 00:52:23.

> *Facilitator Cue:* There is some mild language in this scene.

Coach Carter learns of the players' not attending class. He reemphasizes his expectations and continues to meet with resistance. In this clip, coach begins to challenge his players to think about the vision they have for themselves by asking them what they want and where their priorities might lie.

- *Chapters 14–15:* "Report to the Library." Begins in chapter 14 and continues into chapter 15 ("Real Statistics") of the DVD at approximately 01:21:29 to 01:29:48.

> *Facilitator Cue:* There is some language in these scenes.

Facilitator Cue: If you choose, you can skip the segment between 01:25:00 and 01:27:05. You may also choose to show chapter 16, "Education," to see the additional conflict and challenges the coach faces from the players' parents and the community. *Warning*: There is very strong language in chapter 16.

The coach receives the team's academic progress reports and finds their grades as a whole disturbing. As a result, he locks the gym, cancels practices and an upcoming game, and then challenges the principal and the team about the priorities they have in their lives. When there is no change, he recruits some teachers to provide tutoring to the players.

- *Chapter 18:* "Lockout Vote." Begins in chapter 18 of the DVD at approximately 01:39:16 to 1:44:12.

The lockout of basketball comes to the board of education with a push by the community to vote to end it. Arguments from the community support ending the lockout and go directly against the values that Carter has tried to instill in the program and in his players.

Leadership Lessons from *Coach Carter*

Discussion Questions for "Contract"

1. How does Coach Carter outline his expectations to the team? What is the importance of leaders' expressing their expectations?
2. What are the results of the coach's use of the contract, and how does he address the reaction? How do his reactions relate to effective leadership?

Discussion Questions for "Student Athlete"

1. When the parents react to the coach's contract approach, what leadership behaviors does he exhibit with his reply?
2. As a leader, how would you deal with such a reaction from the crowd or mainstream?

Discussion Questions for "Classroom Performance"

1. In what ways does the coach begin to help students think about their vision?
2. How does a personal vision for one's self translate to a vision that leaders try to have for their groups?

Discussion Questions for "Report to the Library"

1. How does the coach use the expectations he previously set to hold the team accountable? What are some techniques or strategies that leaders can use to hold group members accountable?

2. How does the coach express the ideal of "team" to the group? How does this apply to members of a group?
3. What challenges does the coach face from the principal? In the library, what challenges does the coach face from the players? Consider how the coach responds to those challenges.
   - As a leader, how do you face challenges that come along from others or from situations? What temperament did the coach demonstrate in dealing with these challenges?

Discussion Questions for "Lockout Vote"

1. How does the coach express the values he believes his players need to hold?
   - What reactions does he get from your audience? What reactions do you see in his two players that are sitting in the back of the room?
2. How does the coach address these reactions?

• • •

MOVIE: *THE LION KING*

1994. Director: Roger Allers and Rob Minkoff
Screenplay: Irene Mecchi
Distribution: Buena Vista Pictures Distribution
Rated G

The Five Practices Exhibited in the Selected Scenes of *The Lion King*

- Model the Way (as well as lack of honesty, integrity, and values)
- Inspire a Shared Vision (as well as lack of vision)
- Challenge the Process
- Enable Others to Act (as well as not enabling others)
- Encourage the Heart

Disney's animated musical is about a lion cub that faces struggles, after his father is killed, to become the new leader of the jungle.

Synopsis

The circle of life in the animal kingdom begins with the king, Mufasa, who strives to raise his son, Simba, to be prepared to take the throne. Mufasa's untimely death at the hands of his own brother, Scar, thrusts Simba into a life he is too young to handle. Scar takes over the kingdom and leads it into a horrendous state while Simba rambles throughout the land in search of who he is. As he happens upon new friends that help him find his way back, he develops into the lion king his father always expected and knew he could be. Simba returns to find his place in the circle of life: he takes the reins of the kingdom and restores it to the magical and wonderful land his father had led.

Scene Descriptions

The following descriptions for three scenes in the film illustrate a number of The Five Practices. You can view these scenes as individual clips, stopping to discuss them in between, or watch the whole sequence with discussion afterward. This would be appropriate for program structures such as a class or an ongoing leadership workshop series where you can show the movie in one of your sessions, or have students view the movie on their own time and be prepared to discuss in the leadership session.

- *Chapter 3:* "Father and Son/Morning Report." Begins in chapter 3 of the DVD at approximately 00:08:47 (0 hours, 8 minutes, 47 seconds) to 00:10:02.

Mufasa begins to teach Simba about the role of a (king) leader. He talks about the kingdom (i.e., a leader's group) and what responsibilities leaders have to those who follow him or her.

- *Chapter 14:* "Scar in Command." Begins in chapter 14 of the DVD at approximately 00:49:30 to 00:50:33.

Scar, Mufasa's brother, assumes the role as leader now that Mufasa has been killed and Simba is presumed dead. Scar's temperament and style as leader are much different from Mufasa's and are demonstrated by his actions in this scene.

> *Facilitator Cue:* After some discussion, you can add in chapters 20 and 21 at 01:11:53 to see some physical results of Scar's leadership over the years. At 01:13:13 to 01:15:00, you can see Scar demonstrate more of his leadership behaviors. Pick up again at 01:15:24 to 01:17:12.

- *Chapter 19:* "He Lives in You." Begins in chapter 19 of the DVD at approximately 01:08:05 to 01:09:00.

After having a "visit" from his deceased father, Simba talks with Rafiki about the challenges of going forward and how his past haunts him. Rafiki tells Simba change is good.

Leadership Lessons from *The Lion King*

Discussion Questions for "Father and Son/Morning Report"

1. What is the initial lesson that Mufasa has for Simba regarding the role a leader has?
    - How does Mufasa distinguish between someone who is in charge and thinks he or she is a leader and always get his or her way and one who feels genuine responsibilities to help others become better?

Discussion Questions for "Scar in Command"

1. Scar demonstrates the leader behaviors of a bad (or ineffective) leader. What are they?
2. If you were to exhibit these types of leadership behaviors, list some of the things you would imagine happening to your group.
3. If you continue by showing the scenes in chapter 20 and 21, what other negative and ineffective leadership behaviors do you see in Scar?
4. What evidence of a lack of honesty or integrity do you see in Scar?

Discussion Questions for "He Lives in You"

1. What lessons does Simba realize when talking about his past and the mistakes he has made?
2. Rafiki gives a great example of how we can learn from our past and from our mistakes. What practices does this apply to, and how would you apply this lesson to your work as a leader?

• • •

MOVIE: *GANDHI*

1982. Director: Richard Attenborough
Screenplay: John Briley
Distribution: Columbia Pictures
Rated PG for violence and mild profanity. Minimal occurrences are noted in appropriate scenes

The Five Practices Exhibited in the Selected Scenes of Gandhi

- Model the Way
- Inspire a Shared Vision
- Challenge the Process
- Enable Others to Act
- Encourage the Heart

This movie is about Mohandas (Mahatma) Gandhi as he stages nonviolent protests for the rights of Indians in South Africa and continues on his quest to fight for India's freedom and independence from British rule.

Facilitator Cue: This movie has many scenes that demonstrate The Five Practices. If you have the capacity, we recommend using the entire movie as a teaching lesson.

Synopsis

Mahatma Gandhi rose from a small-time lawyer to become one of the most historically famous leaders of civil rights in the nonviolent movement. He stages a nonviolent and noncooperative campaign that eventually results in India's independence from British rule in the early half of the twentieth century.

Scene Descriptions

The following descriptions for five scenes in the film illustrate a number of The Five Practices. You can view these scenes as individual clips, stopping to discuss them in between, or watch the whole sequence with discussion afterward. This would be appropriate for program structures such as a class or an ongoing leadership workshop series where you can show the movie in one of your sessions or have students view the movie on their own time and be prepared to discuss in the leadership session.

Facilitator Cue: There are no chapter titles in this movie.

- *Chapters 6 and 7:* Begins in chapter 6 and continues into chapter 7 of the DVD at approximately 00:54:55 (0 hours, 54 minutes, 55 seconds) to 00:59:04.

Facilitator Cue: You may continue these scenes onto 01:02:00 to see how Gandhi speaks of his philosophy for how India can gain its independence with a different way of "fighting."

This segment begins with Mr. Jinnah, leader of the Muslim League, speaking to the party congress convention (meeting to address independence from Britain) of the need for India to have home rule from the British. After Gandhi is introduced, he begins to share a vision he has for the people of India. At first, many pay him little attention. But to the previous speaker's chagrin, Gandhi captivates the attention of the crowd and helps them begin to see what their country can be.

Facilitator Cue: Earlier in the film, Mr. Jinnah dismissed Gandhi and tells the leaders to invite him to speak at the convention and then let him "slip off into oblivion."

- *Chapter 10:* Begins in chapter 10 of the DVD at approximately 01:17:15 to 01:20:58.

Gandhi meets with some of the leaders to listen to the most recent British plans to repress India. They discuss the resistance they must use, and Gandhi demonstrates his ideas of resistance.

- *Chapter 13:* Begins in chapter 13 of the DVD at approximately 01:34:34 to 01:37:48.

Gandhi and some of the other leaders meet with the British leadership soon after more than fifteen hundred unarmed Indians are shot by an overzealous general. Although the "British government repudiates the massacre," Gandhi uses that incident as an example of why Britain should no longer rule India. Gandhi states his expectations of the British government for leaving India.

The chapter continues with Gandhi addressing the people of India. He shares more of his vision on how India can free itself from Britain.

- *Chapter 15:* Begins in chapter 15 of the DVD at approximately 01:47:15: to 01:49:05.

After a violent uprising where Indian citizens kill police, Gandhi meets again with his advisors and other leaders. When Gandhi suggests the movement must stop due to the violence, the leaders implore him to continue. He refuses, suggesting he will fast until people return to nonviolent behaviors. This is the beginning of an extended hunger strike by Gandhi.

- *Chapters 17–19:* Begins in chapter 17 of the DVD at approximately 02:04:10: to 02:05:50.

Facilitator Cue: You may continue viewing subsequent chapters (through chapter 19 [2:19:00]) to get the full impact of the salt protest. There is violence in subsequent chapters.

British leaders meet to discuss Gandhi's strategy to manufacture salt for India, a crime under British law, as a form of protest and noncompliance. Gandhi marches 240 miles to the sea, gathering the strength of the people along the way. While the British leaders plan to ignore this movement, they are faced with potential embarrassment from around the world at the movement's success.

Leadership Lessons from *Gandhi*

Discussion Questions for Chapters 6 and 7

1. What images did Gandhi offer up to the congress? When did he begin to capture the attention of the congress with his vision of what India could be?
   - How would you describe the complexity and the simplicity of this speech?
2. How would you share a vision for what your group could be? What do you appeal to with those you lead?

Discussion Questions for Chapter 10

1. What does Gandhi do that demonstrates his values and philosophy of protest?
2. What causes the others to have a greater appreciation for Gandhi's ideas?

Discussion Questions for Chapter 13

1. Describe Gandhi's message to the British. What leadership behaviors and practices did you see exhibited in his message? How did the British react to him face-to-face? Then how did they react when he was out of the room? What impact do you think his message had on them? With whom did he have an impact?
2. As the chapter continues, what difference do you see in Gandhi's message when he addresses the people of India?

> *Facilitator Cue:* Look for how Gandhi appeals to the basic needs and values of the people.

3. What images does Gandhi represent as you see him speak? How can this relate to the work that you do?

Discussion Questions for Chapter 15

1. How does Gandhi reinforce his vision?
2. When a leader Inspires a Shared Vision, what are the behaviors that are critical for a vision to be sustained? Do you see any of those behaviors here?

Discussion and Questions for Chapter 17 (through 19 if viewed)

1. Describe persistence as it relates to a leader's role based on what you have seen in the scenes about the salt protest.
2. As a leader, when and how do you determine the degree of persistence you can tolerate and for what issues, projects, or challenges do you make such decisions?
3. How do (or have) the relationships Gandhi has developed with his advisors, the people of India, and others allow his persistence to be effective?

MODULE 9
Commitment

In module 2, we introduced leadership as an ongoing process that ultimately is about self-development. For students to be leaders, now and in the future, they must commit to do the work required to master the skill. Engineers have computers, painters have brushes and paints, and physicians have medicine. Leaders have only themselves: that is their instrument. Excellence in anything—whether it's music, sports, or academics—requires deliberate practice. Leadership is no exception. Students need to devote time every day to becoming the best leader they can be. Committing to leadership excellence is a personal commitment that begins with exploration of the territory within.

In this module, we provide activities to help students get the deliberate practice they need to continue their journey. We offer ways to continue their exploration within and ways to increase the frequency with which they demonstrate the behaviors that will make them effective, no matter what leadership role they embrace.

Activities

- Values-in-Action Log
- My Year of Leadership
- My Next Personal-Best Experience

• • •

ACTIVITY: VALUES-IN-ACTION LOG

Objectives

Students will be able to:

- Identify actions taken in support of values
- Plan for actions that will align with values
- Establish a pattern of reflection on how their values show up in their lives
- Establish a habit of choosing to demonstrate one's values

Time Required

- 5 to 10 minutes daily

Materials and Equipment

- Values-in-Action log

Process

Facilitator Cue: This activity should take place after participants have engaged in a values identification exercise such as the Values-on-Display activity in module 3.

1. Remind participants that we all should take the opportunity to plan our actions and reflect on them after the fact. Each is very useful, and the Value-in-Action Log can be used in each instance. Exemplary leaders take the time to do both. This activity is designed as a reflective exercise, but you can rewrite the instructions and use it as a planning exercise as well. To use it as a reflective tool, students record in their log an action they took on the day they are completing it that aligned with one of the values they have previously identified.

Facilitator Cue: This can be done on any schedule that makes sense for the group, but the more often, the better.

2. To use the Values-in-Action log as a planning tool, students look ahead and plan action they can take that will align with one of the values they have identified.
3. After they have used the log for twenty-one days, ask the following questions:
   - What value was the easiest to incorporate into your day?
   - Which value was the most difficult to build into your day?
   - Were you more likely to plan something on your own after you used the log as a reflection tool or a planning tool?
   - What does your answer tell you about how you work best?

Reflection and Connection to the Model

This activity is closely aligned to Model the Way because of its focus, but it also provides space to explore some of the important lessons we've learned from our research on The Student Leadership Challenge:

- Leadership is learned.
- Leadership requires deliberate practice.
- Leadership in an ongoing process.
- Leadership is a choice and an aspiration.

Consider asking students these questions over time:

- The Student Leadership Challenge suggests that leadership is learned. Do you believe you have learned to be a more effective leader?
- The Student Leadership Challenge suggests that leadership requires deliberate practice. Do you think the routine of tracking your values in action has provided good practice opportunities?
- The Student Leadership Challenge suggests that leadership is an ongoing process. Based on the ongoing effort to track your values in action, do you believe this is true? What is your evidence?
- Based on the values in action that you have tracked, what choices have you made that show you aspire to become a better leader?

STUDENT WORKSHEET: VALUES-IN-ACTION LOG

Select three top values from a list you have identified in a previous values identification exercise. Capture specific actions you took that you feel demonstrate the value in action.

Value 1:

Value 2:

Value 3:

Date:

Value:

Action:

Date:

Value:

Action:

Date:

Value:

Action:

ACTIVITY: MY YEAR OF LEADERSHIP

Objectives

Students will be able to:

- Identify daily actions that demonstrate leadership
- Reinforce commitment to making leadership behavior a priority, an aspiration, and a choice
- Learn about their capacity to lead

Time Required

- 5 to 10 minutes minimum

Materials and Equipment

- A physical log, notebook, or calendar or a virtual calendar, log, or blog

Process

1. Make a commitment to demonstrate a leadership practice every day for one year.
2. Find a way to record the practice you chose, how you demonstrated that practice, and the result.
3. Find a way to capture that information such as a journal or a blog.
4. Incorporate a monthly note about the process: Is it getting easier? Harder? Are you demonstrating your leadership practices in different settings?
5. Are you demonstrating one practice more than the others?

Reflection and Connection to the Model

This activity is intended to tie directly to the Five Practices of Exemplary Leadership model. It can be done at the behavior level of the Student Leadership Practices Inventory as well, which may be easier to plan. However, there are good things to be gained from having to think about what behavior to demonstrate rather than pulling from a list.

ACTIVITY: MY NEXT PERSONAL-BEST LEADERSHIP EXPERIENCE

Objectives

Students will be able to:

- Proactively plan for success
- Reinforce their commitment to making leadership behavior a priority, an aspiration, and a choice
- Build their capacity to lead

Time Required

- 30 to 45 minutes minimum

Process

Facilitator Cue: This is a good exercise to book-end a workshop or retreat. If students have completed The Personal-Best Leadership Experience activity in module 2, they will be familiar with the type of story that was shared. The goal of this activity is to help create another story of success. Students will create the outline of the story.

1. Have students think about an upcoming opportunity to play a leadership role. Have them write it on the My Next Personal-Best Leadership Experience worksheet.
2. Have them complete as much of the worksheet as possible.
3. When they have gotten as far as they can alone, have them work in small groups of two to three to get the support of their peers to fill in the rest.
4. If this group will not be together again, you can have them close the event with a commitment date. If they will be meeting again, it can be a commitment to share the results with the small group who supported their planning.

Reflection and Connection to the Model

Leadership is an ongoing process of self-development. This activity helps students to formalize their commitment to growing as a leader and to increasing the frequency of personal best leadership experiences.

STUDENT WORKSHEET: MY NEXT PERSONAL-BEST LEADERSHIP EXPERIENCE

1. Identify a success you would like to have as a leader by completing the following sentence:

   When this __________ [e.g., event, project, school year] is complete, I will be celebrating because these things happened (fill in at least three and make them as specific as you can):

   - ____________________
   - ____________________
   - ____________________
   - ____________________
   - ____________________
   - ____________________
   - ____________________
   - ____________________

2. My team will also be celebrating because of what we accomplished. Together we [fill in at least three and make them as specific as you can]:

   - ____________________
   - ____________________
   - ____________________
   - ____________________
   - ____________________
   - ____________________
   - ____________________
   - ____________________

OTHER RESOURCES

The number of resources available to support the ongoing development of your student leaders continues to grow. We have listed a few here and hope that you will go to www.studentleadershipchallenge.com to explore these and other options.

The Student Leadership Challenge, Second Edition

We highly recommend you have your students read *The Student Leadership Challenge* book to deepen their understanding of The Five Practices by learning about other students who demonstrate the leadership behaviors embedded in the model. The book offers evidence from our research and that of others to support our core philosophy that leadership is everyone's business. It provides case examples of young people who demonstrate each practice and prescribes specific recommendations on what people can do to make each practice their own and to continue their development as a leader.

The Student Leadership Practices Inventory

This is a comprehensive leadership development tool designed to help young people measure their leadership behaviors and take action to improve their effectiveness as a leader. It is grounded in the same extensive research as *The Leadership Practices Inventory* (*LPI*), a classic that is used in leadership training, executive development, and graduate-level programs around the world. The *Student LPI* is available in self- and 360-degree assessment formats in paper and online versions.

The Student Leadership Challenge: Facilitation and Activity Guide and *The Student Leadership Challenge: Student Workbook and Personal Leadership Journal*

These two publications offer comprehensive coverage of The Student Leadership Challenge. The *Facilitation and Activity Guide* is intended to guide you in the important role you play in supporting students' development as leaders. We designed it to go beyond the instruction of The Five Practices of Exemplary Leadership model to provide tools for the important work you do: the encouragement and support of students' ongoing journey as developing leaders. *The Student Workbook and Personal Leadership Journal* aligns with the structure of the *Facilitation and Activity Guide* and is designed to deepen students' understanding of The Five Practices at both a conceptual and applied level.

The Leadership Challenge Mobile Tool App

Whether you are new to The Leadership Challenge or an experienced student of The Five Practices of Exemplary Leadership model, this app provides a touch-and-go tool kit of tips and techniques allowing users to put The Five Practices into action using the mobile devices students are most comfortable with. The app is available in the iTunes App Store for use with iPhones or iPads or with the iPod Touch. This portal provides easy access to practice tips, case studies, videos, events, and daily inspiration. It is fully interactive with e-mail, access to Facebook, an RSS news feed, and more.

LPI Action Cards

The LPI Action Cards are designed to help leaders at all levels improve their leadership by developing specific leadership behaviors through guided learning activities. They allow leaders to apply the knowledge they have to case studies and to their own leadership challenges, thereby offering the practice that is required to develop leadership skills. The activities are designed to be used as stand-alone exercises or in conjunction with the LPI or the Student LPI. They can also be used as workshop activities, or as application or follow-up activities.

There is a Facilitator's Guide for the LPI Action Cards with a wealth of activities for the introduction, application, and reinforcement of The Five Practices and the thirty leadership behaviors.

The Leadership Challenge Values Cards

The Leadership Challenge Values Cards can help experienced or aspiring leaders clarify their personal values, as well as to build consensus on shared values that will guide them and their teams in making decisions and taking actions in all situations. Each card is printed with key words such as *creativity, loyalty,* and *teamwork* so that participants can easily identify and record the values that are most meaningful to them.

The *Facilitator's Guide for The Leadership Challenge Values Cards* offers a wealth of activities that will help spark the important conversations about values and their role in effective leadership.

The Student Leadership Challenge Website

This website (www.studentleadershipchallenge.com) has many additional activities, lesson plans, videos, and more. The Resources Section offers quick tips and the newsletter.

Certified Facilitators have access to an additional layer of the website where they can network and share best practices. If you are interested in becoming a Certified Facilitator of The Student Leadership Challenge, go the website and look under "Training."

APPENDIX

Activities Mapped to the Student Leadership Practices Inventory Behaviors

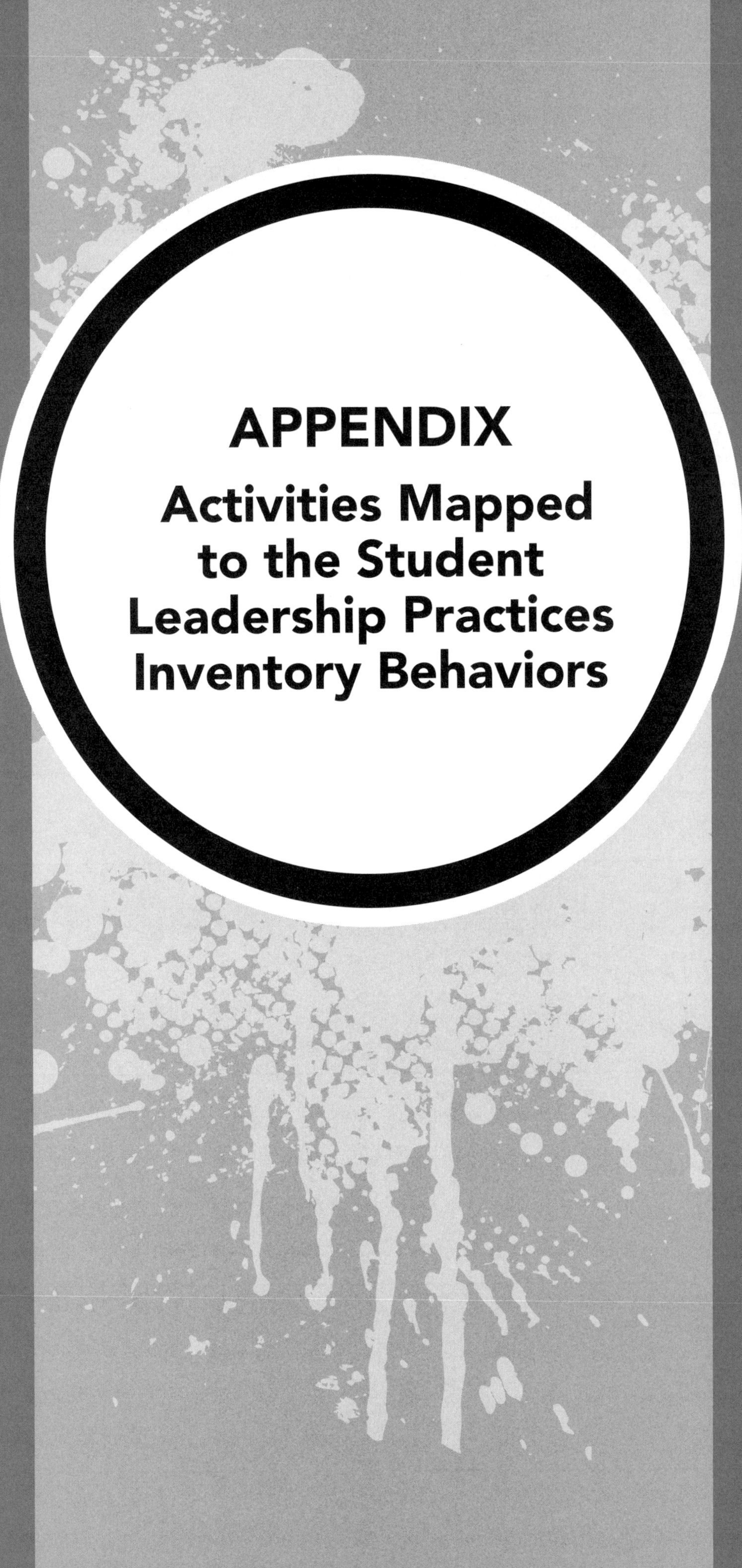

Activities Mapped To The Student Leadership Practices Inventory Behaviors

Model the Way								
Statement #1 "I set a personal example of what I expect from other people." *(Student LPI Report:* "Sets personal example.")	Values on Display	Modeling the Way in Current Events	The Hefferlump	You Want What?	You Can Lead Anywhere		Legacy Day	Vault of Values
Statement #6 "I spend time making sure that people behave consistently with the principles and standards we have agreed upon." (*Student LPI Report:* "Aligns others with principles and standards.")		Modeling the Way in Current Events	The Hefferlump	You Want What?	You Can Lead Anywhere	This We Believe		Vault of Values
Statement #11 "I follow through on the promises and commitments I make." (*Student LPI Report:* "Follows through on promises.")		Modeling the Way in Current Events			You Can Lead Anywhere		Legacy Day	
Statement #16 "I seek to understand how my actions affect other people's performance." *Student LPI Report:* "Seeks feedback about impact of actions.")		Modeling the Way in Current Events	The Hefferlump	You Want What?	You Can Lead Anywhere			
Statement #21 "I make sure that people support the values we have agreed upon." (*Student LPI Report:* "Makes sure people support common values.")		Modeling the Way in Current Events	The Hefferlump	You Want What?	You Can Lead Anywhere	This We Believe		Vault of Values
Statement #26 "I talk about my values and the principles that guide my actions." (*Student LPI Report:* "Talks about values and principles.")	Values on Display	Modeling the Way in Current Events			You Can Lead Anywhere	This We Believe	Legacy Day	Vault of Values

Inspire a Shared Vision								
Statement #2 "I look ahead and communicate what I believe will affect us in the future." (*Student LPI Report:* "Looks ahead and communicates future.")		Word Pictures: Articulating Your Vision	Giving Life to Your Vision by Reframing from What to Why			Vision, Values, and Rock and Roll A Picture Is Worth a Thousand Words	Sum It All Up	Finish the Story
Statement #7 "I describe to others in our organization what we should be capable of accomplishing." (*Student LPI Report:* "Describes ideal capabilities.")		Word Pictures: Articulating Your Vision	Giving Life to Your Vision by Reframing from What to Why			Vision, Values, and Rock and Roll A Picture Is Worth a Thousand Words	Sum It All Up	Finish the Story
Statement #12 "I talk with others about a vision of how things could be even better in the future." (*Student LPI Report:* "Talks about how the future could be better.")			Giving Life to Your Vision by Reframing from What to Why			Vision, Values, and Rock and Roll A Picture Is Worth a Thousand Words	Sum It All Up	Finish the Story
Statement #17 "I talk with others about how their own interests can be met by working toward a common goal." (*Student LPI Report:* "Shows others how their interests can be realized.")	Going Up	Word Pictures: Articulating Your Vision	Giving Life to Your Vision by Reframing from What to Why	Visualize Yourself	Snapshots of Success	Vision, Values, and Rock and Roll A Picture Is Worth a Thousand Words	Sum It All Up	Finish the Story
Statement #22 "I am upbeat and positive when talking about what we can accomplish." (*Student LPI Report:* "Is upbeat and positive.")	Going Up		Giving Life to Your Vision by Reframing from What to Why	Visualize Yourself	Snapshots of Success	Vision, Values, and Rock and Roll A Picture Is Worth a Thousand Words	Sum It All Up	Finish the Story

Statement #27 "I speak with passion about the higher purpose and meaning of what we are doing." (*Student LPI Report:* "Communicates purpose and meaning.")	Going Up		Giving Life to Your Vision by Reframing from What to Why	Visualize Yourself	Snapshots of Success	Vision, Values, and Rock and Roll A Picture Is Worth a Thousand Words	Sum It All Up	Finish the Story
Challenge the Process								
Statement #3 "I look around for ways to develop and challenge my skills and abilities." (*Student LPI Report:* "Challenges skills and abilities.")		"Orientation: The Time of Your Life"—A Skit		This is How We've Always Done It . . . But Let's Try Something Else		Brick Walls Don't Have to Stop You Finish the Story	Planning with the End in Mind	The Six Thinking Hats
Statement #8 "I look for ways that others can try out new ideas and methods." (*Student LPI Report:* "Helps others try out new ideas.")	House of Cards	"Orientation: The Time of Your Life": A Skit	Going, Going, Gone	This is How We've Always Done It . . . But Let's Try Something Else	Turning Big Challenges into Incremental Action Steps	Brick Walls Don't Have to Stop You Finish the Story	Planning with the End in Mind	The Six Thinking Hats
Statement #13 "I search for innovative ways to improve what we are doing." (*Student LPI Report:* "Searches for innovative ways to improve.")	House of Cards	"Orientation: The Time of Your Life"—A Skit	Going, Going, Gone	This is How We've Always Done It . . . But Let's Try Something Else	Turning Big Challenges into Incremental Action Steps		Planning with the End in Mind	The Six Thinking Hats
Statement #18 "When things don't go as we expected, I ask, 'What can we learn from this experience?'" (*Student LPI Report:* "Asks, 'What can we learn?'")	House of Cards					Brick Walls Don't Have to Stop You	Planning with the End in Mind	Six Hats Thinking

Statement #23 "I make sure that big projects we undertake are broken down into smaller and doable portions." (*Student LPI Report:* "Breaks projects into smaller doable parts."		"Orientation: The Time of Your Life"—A Skit			Turning Big Challenges into Incremental Action Steps	Brick Walls Don't Have to Stop You	Planning with the End in Mind	The Six Thinking Hats
Statement #28 "I take initiative in experimenting with the way things can be done." (*Student LPI Report:* "Takes initiative in experimenting.")	House of Cards	"Orientation: The Time of Your Life"—A Skit	Going, Going, Gone	This is How We've Always Done It . . . But Let's Try Something Else	Turning Big Challenges into Incremental Action Steps	Brick Walls Don't Have to Stop You	Planning with the End in Mind	Six Hats Thinking
Enable Others to Act								
Statement #4 "I foster cooperative rather than competitive relationships among people I work with." (*Student LPI Report:* "Fosters cooperative relationships.")	The Walk of Peril (or Indiana Jones's Walk)	The Captains' Dilemma	Tennis Ball Madness	A Picture Is Worth a Thousand Words	Populating a New Planet	A Leader's Walk of Trust	Capture the Dragon	The Six Thinking Hats
Statement #9 "I actively listen to diverse points of view." (*Student LPI Report:* "Actively listens to diverse viewpoints.")	The Walk of Peril (or Indiana Jones's Walk)	The Captains' Dilemma	Tennis Ball Madness	A Picture Is Worth a Thousand Words	Populating a New Planet		Capture the Dragon	Help Is on the Way
Statement #14 "I treat others with dignity and respect." (*Student LPI Report:* "Treats others with respect.")	The Walk of Peril (or Indiana Jones's Walk)	The Captains' Dilemma	Tennis Ball Madness	A Picture Is Worth a Thousand Words	Populating a New Planet	A Leader's Walk of Trust	Capture the Dragon	Help Is on the Way
Statement #19 "I support the decisions that other people make on their own." (*Student LPI Report:* "Supports decisions other people make.")	The Walk of Peril (or Indiana Jones's Walk)	The Captains' Dilemma	Tennis Ball Madness	A Picture Is Worth a Thousand Words	Populating a New Planet		Capture the Dragon	Help Is on the Way

Statement #24 "I give others a great deal of freedom and choice in deciding how to do their work." (*Student LPI Report:* "Gives people choice about how to do their work.")	The Walk of Peril (or Indiana Jones's Walk)	The Captains' Dilemma	Tennis Ball Madness	A Picture Is Worth a Thousand Words	Populating a New Planet	A Leader's Walk of Trust		Help Is on the Way
Statement #29 "I provide opportunities for others to take on leadership responsibilities." (*Student LPI Report:* "Provides leadership opportunities for others.")	The Walk of Peril (or Indiana Jones's Walk)	The Captains' Dilemma	Tennis Ball Madness	A Picture Is Worth a Thousand Words	Populating a New Planet		Capture the Dragon	Help Is on the Way
Encourage the Heart								
Statement #5 "I praise people for a job well done." (*Student LPI Report:* "Praises people.")	Compliment Swap	Praise	Identifying Individual Recognition Tactics	Encourage the Heart Party Time with Your Group	Recognition Car Wash	Recognition Speed Dating	Good Vibrations	Web of Yarn
Statement #10 "I encourage others as they work on activities and programs." (*Student LPI Report:* "Encourages others.")	Compliment Swap	Praise	Identifying Individual Recognition Tactics	Encourage the Heart Party Time with Your Group				
Statement #15 "I express appreciation for the contributions people make." (*Student LPI Report:* "Expresses appreciation for people's contributions.")	Compliment Swap	Praise	Identifying Individual Recognition Tactics	Encourage the Heart Party Time with Your Group	Recognition Car Wash	Recognition Speed Dating	Good Vibrations	
Statement #20 "I make it a point to publicly recognize people who show commitment to shared values." (*Student LPI report:* "Publicly recognizes alignment with values.")		Praise	Identifying Individual Recognition Tactics	Encourage the Heart Party Time with Your Group	Recognition Car Wash			Web of Yarn

Statement #25 "I find ways for us to celebrate accomplishments." (*Student LPI Report:* "Celebrates accomplishments.")			Identifying Individual Recognition Tactics	Encourage the Heart Party Time with Your Group		Recognition Speed Dating	Good Vibrations	Web of Yarn
Statement #30 "I make sure that people are creatively recognized for their contributions." (*Student LPI Report:* "Creatively recognizes people's contributions.")	Compliment Swap		Identifying Individual Recognition Tactics	Encourage the Heart Party Time with Your Group	Recognition Car Wash	Recognition Speed Dating	Good Vibrations	Web of Yarn

ACKNOWLEDGMENTS

You can't do it alone. It's one of the truths about leading. It's equally true about writing. While the tasks of writing are often lonely and tedious, the pleasures of interacting with our colleagues are always fun and uplifting. One of the great joys of writing a book is the opportunity to work with scores of talented, dedicated, and inspiring people. We are profoundly grateful to them, and we cherish the opportunity go to say "thank you" to all who have joined us on this journey.

This *Activity Book* has been made possible because of the generosity of the nearly forty colleagues who have contributed to this volume. These are activities that they have all used in programs they've conducted with students and other leaders, and we are grateful that they have shared their experiences with us. Thank you all for making your work available to our readers around the world.

Thank you to the thousands of students we've worked with over the years. You inspire us and bring us hope. You give us immense confidence that our future is held in capable hands and generous hearts.

As always, Jim and Barry offer their deepest appreciation to their immediate loved ones—to Tae and Nick, and to Jackie and Amanda and Darryl. You bring great joy into our lives. We have witnessed—and experienced— your extraordinary feats of leadership; you have taught us more than we can ever share. Beth extends her gratitude to Tom, Georgia, and Evan, and Gary thanks his daughter Savannah Morgan-Muskin, Sheri, man's best friend, Dell, and God for the support and inspiration to be a part of writing this book with Jim, Barry, and Beth.

We cannot fully express our appreciation to Leslie Stephen, our developmental editor, our collaborator, our cheerleader, and our "Dream Weaver" on this book and many others we have worked on. Leslie generously and graciously kept us focused over many long hours, and endlessly offered encouragement and a calm presence. Leslie, you are a gem!

From the start, Erin Null, editor, Higher and Adult Education, championed this project with her colleagues at Jossey-Bass, a Wiley brand. She moved us forward with caring leadership and a gracious guiding hand. Without Erin's passion, persuasiveness, and professionalism this new edition would never have been written. Thank you, Erin, for believing in us and in the value of this project. And when Erin took maternity leave in the final months of writing, Alison Knowles, assistant editor, took charge and got us across the finish line with confidence and competence. Other Wiley team members contributed greatly to the success of this edition: Adrian Morgan, cover design; Aneesa Davenport, marketing manager; Cathy Mallon, production editor; Bev Miller, copy editor; and Paul Foster, publisher.

Larry Mannolini, Cheryl Kalberer, Gina McClure, and Denise Knight added their valuable perspectives, enabling us to make important and significant improvements. Their sage advice and wise counsel improved both the substance and clarity of the final version. We deeply appreciate their insights and nudging.

We wrote this book, as we have each of our books, in order to liberate the leader that lies within each of us. That's our mission and our passion. Each and every one of us matters. Each and every one of us makes a difference. The real challenge for all of us is to continue to make the difference we intended. Live your life forward.

AUTHORS AND CONTRIBUTORS

THE AUTHORS

Jim Kouzes and **Barry Posner** have been working together for more than thirty years, studying leaders, researching leadership, conducting leadership development seminars, and serving as leaders themselves in various capacities. They are coauthors of the award-winning, best-selling book *The Leadership Challenge*, now in its fifth edition. Since the publication of the first edition in 1987, *The Leadership Challenge* has sold more than two million copies worldwide and is available in more than twenty-two languages. It has won numerous awards, including the Critics' Choice Award from the nation's book review editors and the James A. Hamilton Hospital Administrators' Book of the Year Award. It was selected as one of the top ten books on leadership in *The 100 Best Business Books of All Time*. *The Student Leadership Challenge*, in its first edition, has been used in leadership classes and programs in educational institutions and organizations around the globe with college students and youth development organizations. Jim and Barry have coauthored more than a dozen other award-winning leadership books, including *Finding the Courage to Lead*; *Great Leadership Creates Great Workplaces*; *Making Extraordinary Things Happen in Asia: Applying The Five Practices of Exemplary Leadership*; *Credibility: How Leaders Gain and Lose It, Why People Demand It*; *The Truth about Leadership: The No-Fads, Heart-of-the-Matter Facts You Need to Know*; *A Leader's Legacy*; *Encouraging the Heart: A Leader's Guide to Rewarding and Recognizing Others*; and *The Academic Administrator's Guide to Exemplary Leadership*. They developed the highly acclaimed *Leadership Practices Inventory (LPI)*, a 360-degree questionnaire for assessing leadership behavior, one of the most widely used leadership assessment instruments in the world. The student version of the LPI has been used by more than 150,000 students. Over six hundred doctoral dissertations and academic papers have been based on their The Five Practices of Exemplary Leadership model.

Among the honors and awards that Jim and Barry have received is the American Society for Training and Development's highest award for their Distinguished Contribution to Workplace Learning and Performance. They have been named Management/Leadership Educators of the Year by the International Management Council; ranked by *Leadership Excellence* magazine in the top twenty on its list of the Top 100 Thought Leaders; named among the 50 Top Coaches in the nation (according to *Coaching for Leadership*); included among the Top 100 Thought Leaders in Trustworthy Business Behavior by Trust Across America; and listed among *HR Magazine*'s Most Influential International Thinkers.

Jim and Barry are frequent keynote speakers, and each has conducted leadership development programs for hundreds of organizations, including Alberta Health Services, Amazon, Apple, ARCO, AT&T, Australia Institute of Management, Australia Post, Bank of America, Bose, Charles Schwab, Chevron, Cisco Systems, Clorox, Community Leadership Association, Conference Board of Canada, Consumers Energy, Deloitte Touche, Dorothy Wylie Nursing and Health Leaders Institute, Dow Chemical, Egon Zehnder International, Federal Express, Genentech, Google, Gymboree, HP, IBM, Jobs DR-Singapore, Johnson & Johnson, Kaiser Foundation Health Plans and Hospitals, Intel, Itau Unibanco, L. L. Bean, Lawrence Livermore National Labs, Lucile Packard Children's Hospital, Merck, Motorola, NetApp, Northrop Grumman, Novartis, Oakwood Temporary Housing, Oracle, Petronas, Roche Bioscience, Siemens, 3M, Toyota, United Way, USAA, Verizon, VISA, the Walt Disney Company, and Westpac. They have lectured at over seventy college and university campuses.

•••

Jim Kouzes is the Dean's Executive Fellow of Leadership, Leavey School of Business at Santa Clara University, and lectures on leadership around the world to corporations, governments, and nonprofits. He is a highly regarded leadership scholar and an experienced executive; the *Wall Street Journal* cited him as one of the twelve best executive educators in the United States. In 2010, Jim received the Thought Leadership Award from the Instructional Systems Association, the most prestigious award given by the trade association of training and development industry providers. He was listed as one of *HR Magazine*'s Most Influential International Thinkers for 2010–2012, named one of the 2010–2013 Top 100 Thought Leaders in Trustworthy Business Behavior by Trust Across America, and ranked by *Leadership Excellence* magazine as number sixteen on its list of the Top 100 Thought Leaders. In 2006, Jim was presented with the Golden Gavel, the highest honor awarded by Toastmasters International. He served as president, CEO, and chairman of the Tom Peters Company from 1988 through 1999 and prior to that led the Executive Development Center at Santa Clara University (1981–1987). Jim founded the Joint Center for Human Services Development at San Jose State University (1972–1980) and was on the staff of the School of Social Work, The University of Texas. His career in training and development began in 1969 when he conducted seminars for Community Action Agency staff and volunteers in the War on Poverty. Following graduation from Michigan State University (BA degree with honors in political science), he served as a Peace Corps volunteer (1967–1969). Jim can be reached at jim@kouzes.com.

• • •

Barry Posner is the Accolti Endowed Professor of Leadership at the Leavey School of Business, Santa Clara University, where he served as dean of the school for twelve years (1997–2009). He has been a distinguished visiting professor at Hong Kong University of Science and Technology, Sabanci University (Istanbul), and the University of Western Australia. At Santa Clara he has received the President's Distinguished Faculty Award, the School's Extraordinary Faculty Award, and several other teaching and academic honors. An internationally renowned scholar and educator, Barry is author or coauthor of more than a hundred research and practitioner-focused articles. He currently serves on the editorial boards for *Leadership and Organizational Development Journal* and the *International Journal of Servant-Leadership.* In 2011, he received the Outstanding Scholar Award for Career Achievement from the *Journal of Management Inquiry.*

Barry received his BA with honors in political science from the University of California, Santa Barbara; his MA in public administration from The Ohio State University; and his PhD in organizational behavior and administrative theory from the University of Massachusetts, Amherst. Having consulted with a wide variety of public and private sector organizations around the globe, Barry also works at a strategic level with a number of community-based and professional organizations, currently sitting on the board of directors of EMQ FamiliesFirst. He has served previously on the boards of the American Institute of Architects, Big Brothers/Big Sisters of Santa Clara County, Center for Excellence in Nonprofits, Junior Achievement of Silicon Valley and Monterey Bay, Public Allies, San Jose Repertory Theater, Sigma Phi Epsilon Fraternity, and both publicly traded and start-up companies. Barry can be reached at bposner@scu.edu.

• • •

Beth High is an author, organizational consultant, program designer, coach, keynote speaker, and Certified Master Facilitator for The Leadership Challenge. Her work in these areas has allowed her to develop a strong client list from a variety of sectors, including Capital One; Girls, Inc.; John Wiley and Sons, England and Dubai; KalTire Canada; North Carolina Department of Transportation; SAS and SAS Asia Pacific; Saudi Arabia Ministry of Education; Western Union; University of Arkansas; University of North Carolina School of Government; University of North Carolina School of Business; and VF Jeanswear. She is president of High Road Consulting, a leadership development company based in Chapel Hill, North Carolina.

This body of work serves as the foundation for most of the programs Beth leads. She has produced The Leadercast Series, a podcast series with authors Jim Kouzes and Barry Posner, and developed a Jossey-Bass Certification Program for educators interested in developing programs based on *The Student Leadership Challenge.* The unique blended learning approach for this program allowed Beth to create the platform on which The Leadership Challenge Workshop Online was subsequently created. This work resulted in the creation of her partner company HRCPartners, which focuses solely on the development and implementation of The Leadership Challenge Workshop Online and the FollowThruOnline product platforms.

Beth regularly delivers the Leadership Challenge Workshop in a variety of formats and consults with companies globally on how to incorporate The Five Practices model into their existing leadership programs. She has designed facilitator certification programs in South America and the Middle East, helping regional facilitators embrace the model in their unique cultures. She is a coauthor of *The Student Leadership Challenge Facilitation and Activity Guide* and *The Student Leadership Challenge Student Workbook and Personal Leadership Journal.* Having completed an MEd in instructional design and educational media at the University of North Carolina, Chapel Hill, she is committed to top-quality design of programs that explore new technologies while addressing the unique learning and development needs of the audience. Her expertise enables her to consult, design, and deliver long-format programs (of eighteen to twenty-four months) built around virtual centers and using a blended learning approach. Beth and her team work closely with clients to customize program content and capture the appropriate data these sites provide. These centers allow participants to have the extended practice essential for building skills and provide the program owners with evidence of ROI from the training. Beth can be reached at highroadconsulting@gmail.com.

•••

Gary M. Morgan has taught or developed student leadership courses and programs at universities of all sizes for the past twenty years. He has served as a dean, director, and faculty member at campuses with enrollments ranging from twelve hundred to fifty-three thousand students and directed programs or services in student leadership, student activities and programming, student government, Greek life, residence life, orientation, the student union, judicial affairs, graduate schools and graduate student life, volunteer and community services, and many other areas. He has always held positions that had a focus of developing students as leaders. In addition to his college-level work, he has developed leadership education programs for high school students in Upward Bound and recently created a summer-long leadership program for foster youth for an Orlando, Florida, community organization.

Gary received a BS degree in communication studies (radio/TV/film) from Northern Illinois University and an MA degree in higher education-college student personnel from Bowling Green State University. He completed the doctoral course work and exam requirements for the PhD in higher education administration at the University of South Carolina. He is a coauthor of *The Student Leadership Challenge Facilitation and Activity Guide* and *The Student Leadership Challenge Student Workbook and Personal Leadership Journal*; a certified facilitator for *The Leadership Challenge* and *The Student Leadership Challenge*; and the founder and CEO of the Student Leadership Excellence Academy and the Leadership Excellence Academy. He is a member of the American College Personnel Association, Student Affairs Administrators in Higher Education, American Society for Training and Development, International Leadership Association, and the National Clearinghouse for Leadership Programs. Gary can be contacted at gary@student-leader.com.

THE CONTRIBUTORS

Jerry Alva is associate vice president for student affairs at Texas A&M International University; he is a Certified Facilitator of The Student Leadership Challenge.

•••

Katie Burke is the assistant director of leadership education and development at Florida Atlantic University in Boca Raton, Florida. She is also a Certified Facilitator of The Student Leadership Challenge.

•••

Robert P. Carskadon, EdD, CPC, is president of Carskadon Associates in Santa Clarita, California.

•••

Angie Vyverberg Chaplin is a Certified Master of The Leadership Challenge and a Certified Facilitator of The Student Leadership Challenge. In addition to her responsibilities as a manager for two outreach centers at Hawkeye Community College, Waterloo, Iowa, she serves learners and leaders at all levels through customized leadership development solutions driven by The Five Practices of Exemplary Leadership.

•••

Mason Chock is the president of Kaua'i Team Challenge (Kupu A'e) and the former executive director of Leadership Kaua. He is a Certified Facilitator of the Student Leadership Challenge and a Certified Master of The Leadership Challenge.

• • •

Scott Dover is a vice president for a medical billing company and football coach at St. Edward High School in Lakewood, Ohio.

• • •

Matthew Eriksen is a professor of management and a director of the Leadership Fellows Program at Providence College.

• • •

Leah Flynn is the assistant dean and director for student leadership and engagement at MIT. She directs the Office of Student Activities and has overarching responsibilities for leadership programs, multicultural programs, LGBT initiatives, and programming for women.

• • •

Rebecca Ford is the editorial program coordinator for higher and adult education at Jossey-Bass in San Francisco. She is a Certified Facilitator of The Student Leadership Challenge.

• • •

R. T. Good, EdD, is a professor of management and associate dean for the Harry F. Byrd Jr. School of Business at Shenandoah University in Winchester, Virginia. He also maintains a private consulting practice.

• • •

Craig Haptonstall is is a vice president for a medical billing company and football coach at St. Edward High School in Lakewood, Ohio.

• • •

Jean McClellan-Holt is the assistant director for sport clubs and summer camps with the Recreation and Wellness Department at Old Dominion University in Norfolk, Virginia.

• • •

Elizabeth Housholder is the assistant dean for civic engagement at Widener University in Chester, Pennsylvania.

• • •

Stephanie Howeth is is director of the Community Engagement and Leadership Center at Southern Methodist University in Dallas, Texas.

• • •

Kelly C. Jordan, PhD, is the dean of students at Holy Cross College in Notre Dame, Indiana. He works extensively with student leadership development as a scholar, educator, and consultant and also teaches a leadership studies minor that he designed.

• • •

Andrea Junso is the director of campus activities at Gustavus Adolphus College in St. Peter, Minnesota, and uses *The Student Leadership Challenge* in her work with the Campus Activities Board and students in ongoing leadership development program.

• • •

Kimberly Hendricks La Grange is a management instructor and director of the Meis Student Development Center in the Scott College of Business at Indiana State University. She is also the principal consultant with Prime Resources, a human resource consulting firm specializing in organizational development and employee training.

• • •

Natalie Loeb is the founder of Loeb Consulting Group. She is an executive coach and facilitator with over twenty years of experience in employee relations, training program design, and facilitation and executive coaching.

• • •

Lawrence P. Mannolini III is director of student programs and leadership development at Lycoming College in Williamsport, Pennsylvania, and a Certified Facilitator of The Student Leadership Challenge.

• • •

Jean McClellan-Holt is the assistant director for sport clubs and summer camps with the Recreation and Wellness Department at Old Dominion University in Norfolk, Virginia.

• • •

Lori McClurg teaches leadership at the Jeffrey S. Raikes School of Computer Science and Management at the University of Nebraska, Lincoln.

• • •

Andrew Moyer is the director of student involvement at Delaware Valley College, where he oversees leadership development and campus life programs. He earned a master's degree in higher education from the University of South Carolina.

• • •

Reba Noel, MEd, is the coordinator of student engagement programs at Langara College in Vancouver, British Columbia.

• • •

Amy Pehrson is the assistant director for vocation and integrative learning and the alumni mentoring program coordinator in the Center for Servant Leadership at Gustavus Adolphus College in St. Peter, Minnesota. Her primary responsibilities include cocurricular leadership development courses and opportunities and developing mentoring programs that pair current students with Gustavus alumni.

• • •

Kurt Penner is a faculty member at Kwantlen Polytechnic University in Vancouver, British Columbia. He is with the Department of Student Life and Development, overseeing new student orientation and student leadership programs.

• • •

Cameron Potter is the principal of the Dream Center Academy, an experiential, adventure-based leadership development high school in Los Angeles.

• • •

Cliff Raphael is an instructor of leadership and geography at the College of New Caledonia, Prince George, British Columbia, Canada.

• • •

Vanessa Schoenherr, MA, is a student development and engagement leader at Ashford University and provides unique and traditional campus experiences to nontraditional online students.

• • •

Aysen Ulupinar-Butzer is the coordinator of cocurricular programs and activities at the University of Akron.

• • •

Clint Whitson is is director of student life and development at Ivy Tech Community College—Central Indiana.

• • •

Melanie Young, MSEd, is a career counselor, academic advisor, transfer student support advisor, national student exchange coordinator, and adjunct instructor at the University of Tennessee at Martin Student Success Center.